The Truth about Cottages

The
Truth about
COTTAGES

John Woodforde

Fifty types of cottage
specially drawn by
Bertha Stamp

Routledge & Kegan Paul
London and Henley

First published 1969
by Routledge & Kegan Paul Ltd
39 Store Steet, London, WC1E 7DD, and
Broadway House, Newtown Road,
Henley-on-Thames, Oxon, RG9 1EN
Reprinted and first published as a paperback
in 1979
Reprinted in 1980
© *J. Woodforde 1969*
Phototypeset by
BAS Printers Limited, Wallop, Hampshire
Printed in Great Britain by
Ebenezer Baylis & Son Ltd
The Trinity Press
Worcester, and London

ISBN 0 7100 6627 9 (c)

ISBN 0 7100 0165 7 (p)

Contents

Acknowledgements

I should like to express my gratitude to Mr A. P. Baggs, F.S.A., of the Royal Commission on Historical Monuments, for reading the typescript of Part II and making most valuable comments. I am also grateful for help and encouragement from Mr T. W. Harrison, L.R.I.B.A., Mr Douglas Matthews of the London Library, the staff of the R.I.B.A. Library, the Secretary of the Society for the Protection of Ancient Buildings and the Assistant Secretary of the Council for the Preservation of Rural England. My wife has helped me on points of English history.

B. Weinreb Ltd. kindly supplied the illustrations on pages 4, 16, 20 and 24, the Mary Evans Picture Library those on pages 3, 11, 41 and 57 and the British Museum those on pages 13, 18, and 40. Books, journals and other publications quoted or referred to are named in the text and appear in italics in the index. The only exception is an unpublished study of the English farmhouse by Eileen Spiegel, which I have been very glad to read in typescript at the R.I.B.A. Library.

J.W.

Inside every Englishman is a villager struggling to get out with such success that scarcely a dank hovel remains in the remotest hamlet that has not by now been turned into a gadget-happy country cottage, a Jaguar resting where the privy used to be. Even when the imprisoned cottager can't break out he shuts his eyes and, deep in the heart of Bermondsey or Brum, pretends to be a cottager. . . .

Elspeth Huxley, *The Sunday Times*, 15 December 1968

A timber-framed Suffolk pair being dismantled. Note the importance of the central chimney stack. Photograph by the author, 1968.

Part One

The Story of Cottage Life

I

Alas!
How Strong they Smell

In 1839 it was suggested by the House of Lords that the state of
the nation's rural cottages might have something to do with an
annual death toll from fevers twice as great as the slaughter
suffered by the allied armies at Waterloo. The Poor Law Commissioners were required to collect evidence from sanitary
officials. Their *Report on the Sanitary Condition of the Labouring
Population*, presented to the Home Secretary in 1842, is a mono-
tonous catalogue of scabrous floors, heaps of ordure, open sewers,
polluted wells and windows stuffed with rags. It should have
convinced the Lords they were right.

A doctor at Tranent described the single-room cottage in which
the father of a young family died from typhus:

> I remember the horse stood at the back of the bed. The
> stench was dreadful. In addition to the horse, there were the
> fowls roosting on the tops of the bedsteads, and I think the
> family was not under ten souls . . . where there are many
> children it is common for 10 or 12 people to inhabit one
> apartment.

A Leighton Buzzard witness said that three or four whole families
often occupied the same cottage sleeping room, which was not
separated from the day room. Some of the hundreds of sanitary
officials applied to seemed even more concerned about the mixed
sleeping than about leaking roofs and 'accumulations of filth by
the door'. One apparently believed himself in the presence of
hardened promiscuity when he witnessed at a miner's cottage a
boy dressing in front of a girl:

It was in the afternoon, when a young man, one of the sons, came downstairs in his shirt and stood before the fire where a very decently-dressed female was sitting. The son asked his mother for a clean shirt, and on its being given to him, very deliberately threw off the shirt he had on, and after warming the clean one, put it on.

No kind of legislative remedy followed the 1842 Report; but these were the days of laissez-faire policies and no one, least of all the Commissioners themselves, seriously expected much action. It can be said, though, that the year 1842 – when permanent income tax began, when factory hours for women were reduced to twelve a day – was the year in which the Government first fully realized that at least three-quarters of all rural labourers' cottages were slums.

Official reports became numerous, and all were lists of horrors. Their most important effect was to shame bad landlords and to stimulate voluntary enterprise. The *Builder* magazine, founded in 1842, began printing designs for cottages, a service it continued for about forty years. Prince Albert concerned himself seriously with problems of cottage sanitation. At the Great Exhibition of 1851 he exhibited designs for a block of four model cottages, and a few years later saw to the building, at his own expense, of fifty-eight such cottages on the outskirts of Windsor. It is ironical that he himself died of typhus picked up, it is believed, from leaking cesspools beneath the floors of Windsor Castle.

But satisfactory plumbing was rare until after the turn of the century. When a new lavatory was begun at Buckingham Palace in about 1840 – it was over Queen Victoria's bedroom – the workmen connected the drain to a rainwater pipe which discharged itself on the leads in front of the Queen's dressing-room window. The smart water-closets of the rich could pave the way to fevers, while sensibly managed earth-closets were safe; for it was not the gases that brought disease, as was then thought, but organisms reaching foodstuffs by way of the human hand or vermin.

For the majority of the ruling classes, infected with a new cult of romanticism and mediaeval revivalism, broken-down cottages and their underfed inhabitants were accepted in the 1840s and long after as desirable ornaments of the countryside. Water-colour sketching was becoming the rage for ladies, and the scenes depicted

Romanticized cheerlessness in what seems to be a Victorian cottage in the 'old English' style. A contemporary engraving by S. Russell.

Thatched hovels in nooks of leaves — ornaments of the countryside c. 1800. Contemporary engravings by J. T. Smith, 1797.

4

were seldom thought complete without a thatched hovel, prefer-
ably in a nook of leaves; the ladies studied examples published by
Francis Stevens 'to yield instruction and amusement to those who
delight in contemplating the rural beauties of our isle'. All
admired the idealized landscapes-with-cottages by Birkett Foster
and the poetry of Felicia Dorothea Hemans:

> The cottage homes of England!
> By thousands on her plains,
> They are smiling o'er the silvery brooks
> And round the hamlet fanes.

These lines were widely read in the collected edition of Mrs
Hemans's poems brought out in 1838. It was not till many years
later that a parody of them appeared in *Punch*:

> The cottage homes of England,
> Alas! How strong they smell;
> There's fever in the cesspool
> And sewage in the well.

The cottage homes of Colerne, delighting the eye of travellers
along the Great Western road on account of their gaily romantic
appearance on the top of a hill, had little to recommend them on
closer inspection. Indeed the impression gained after climbing
the hill for the first time was sickening, according to the medical
officer for Chippenham. He reported to the Poor Law Commissioners on Colerne's

> filth, the dilapidated buildings and the squalid appearance
> of the majority of the lower orders . . . During three years'
> attendance on the poor of this district I have never known
> the small-pox, scarlatina, or the typhus fever to be absent.

The reality of the thatched cottage did not tarnish a cherished
image of a place of contentment and the healthy virtuous life; and
the ideal, according to William Howitt in 1838, gave 'origin to
some of the sweetest paradises in the world – the cottages of the
wealthy and the tasteful'.[1] Some of the paradises were most
substantial. Robert Southey, spotting inverted snobbery in the
attitudes of the wealthy, wrote these harsh lines in *The Devil's Walk*:

---

[1] *The Rural Life of England*, 1838.

A cottage in the Italian style. J. C. Loudon commented that 'this dwelling would produce a very good effect, and might serve for one of those which a recent writer in the Mechanics Magazine *recommends to be substituted for mile-stones along the public roads of Great Britain. To the cottages so placed, he proposes to attach large gardens; and those, with the cottage are to serve as models for neatness and order . . . to the agricultural labourers in the vicinity. The occupier of the cottage is to sit rent-free, on condition of keeping the sides and fences of one mile of road neat and orderly, and as free from weeds and all obstructions as the approach road in a gentleman's park; a labour which might occupy him 50 or 60 days in the year.' From J. C. Loudon's* Encyclopaedia of Cottage Farm and Villa Architecture, *1833.*

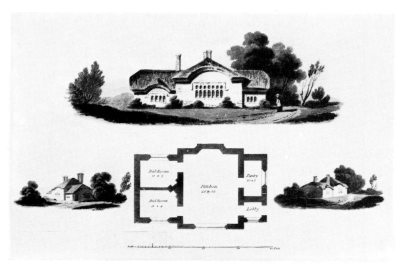

A cottage suitable for the gentry, with a landscaped garden. Without such a garden, according to Elsam, 'rural building hath but few charms'. From Richard Elsam's Hints for Improving the Condition of the Peasantry, *1816.*

6

He passed a cottage with a double coach-house,
  A cottage of gentility!
And he owned with a grin
  That his favourite sin
Is pride that apes humility.

Cottages of gentility, more or less affectedly rustic and equipped for use by the gentry, were familiar sights by the end of the eighteenth century. Jane Austen's Barton Cottage in *Sense and Sensibility* (1811) is an example; it had four principal bedrooms and two garrets, and it accommodated the servants and Miss Dashwood's pianoforte. Mrs Dashwood found fault with its shape for too much resembling that of a house:

> As a cottage it was defective, for the building was regular, the roof was tiled, the window shutters were not painted green, nor were the walls covered with honeysuckles. A narrow passage led directly through the house into the garden behind. On each side of the entrance was a sitting room, about sixteen feet square; and beyond them were the offices and the stairs.

In another novel, *Persuasion*, Jane Austen refers to a farmhouse that had been 'elevated into a cottage' – that is, made suitable for the gentry: it had a verandah, French windows and a pretty drawing room.

Cottage residences shaped to look becomingly rustic grew large enough towards the end of the nineteenth century to hold four domestic servants. At the beginning of the twentieth century, weekend cottages might have eight bedrooms, three sitting-rooms and a couple of bathrooms. Misapplication of the word cottage accounts for it being used today for the substantial half-timber houses of the yeoman farmers. The word retains in this book the sense it has had since Chaucer's time, a small dwelling less in size than the house of a farmer. Three bedrooms are regarded as the maximum.

2

Housed Beggars

Before the eighteenth century the housing of the peasantry was a matter which few people troubled to think about; and labourers' cottages of the sort familiar today did not exist. Cottages were huts and, according to Bacon, all cottagers were housed beggars. He could justify the description by the fact that even peasants with the rank of petty freeholder were subsidized from time to time by charity, thieving or poor relief.

Cottagers and paupers were still being lumped together in Gregory King's statistical survey of England and Wales, compiled in 1688. In this document, the earliest of its kind, King estimated that out of a population of about $5\frac{1}{2}$ million there were 400,000 families who fell into the 'cottagers and paupers' category. He also estimated that over half of the population had expenses greater than their earnings and were thus, in his view, 'decreasing the wealth of the nation'. The submerged majority included labouring people and out-servants, 1,300,000; cottagers and paupers, 1,300,000; common seamen and soldiers, 220,000; vagrants, 30,000. There is of course no way of gauging the accuracy of King's figures, which were partly based on returns of the hearth tax, but his population estimate of $5\frac{1}{2}$ million has been confirmed by later investigators.

Poverty fell to many who were outside the categories given. The standard of living of the small farmers for example – some 750,000 people with an average family income of £44 a year and an expenditure of £42 10s – was considerably lower than that of shopkeepers, tradesmen and artisans. The distresses of the small farmer are described in a late seventeenth-century pamphlet, *The Poor Husband-*

man's Advocate to Rich, Racking Landlords, by Richard Gregory.[1]
Their lot, he says, is harder than that of their own servants who know
their work and wages and are troubled by no cares about paying
rent, the loss of corn and the rotting of sheep in unfavourable
weather. 'They cannot afford to eat their eggs or their fruit but
must make money of all . . . He is a rich man that can afford to
eat a joint of fresh meat once in a month or a fortnight.' However,
Gregory is careful to make exceptions and explains that he is
writing not of all farmers but only of the 'rackt poor', who are
nevertheless the more numerous.

In the sixteenth and seventeenth centuries, 'cottage' meant
either a one-room structure of mud (a universal building material)
with reeds laid on branches for a roof, or else a weak timber
structure with the framework filled in with mud. Many a small
farmer lived in the latter kind, with perhaps an outshut extension.
Joseph Hall, a seventeenth-century bishop of Exeter and Norwich,
thus described the typical cottage of his day:

> Of one bay's[2] breadth, God Wot, a silly cote
> Whose thatched spars are furred with sluttish soot,
> A whole inch thick, shining like blackmoor's brows
> Through smoke that through the headlesse barrel blows . . .

Heating and cooking was by a bonfire on the bare earth floor, its
smoke filtering out by degrees through the roof or through holes
in the walls known as 'wind eyes'. These windows were commonly
formed of Hall's 'headlesse' barrels – that is, barrels or baskets
with the bottom knocked out and built into mud walls. Water was
taken from wells, ditches and ponds.

The substantial oak-framed 'cottages' of which thousands
survive today were by no means mere cottages to their first inhabitants. They might have only two bedrooms; but they were the
residences of men of means – sheep farmers, merchants, tradesmen
– men of the new yeoman class who owed their prosperity to
exporting wool. Since the sixteenth century, landowners had been
grazing more and ploughing less; they had found that instead of
scratching up a living with the aid of bands of peasants they could

---

[1] Quoted by Dorothy M. George, *England in Transition*, 1931.
[2] A bay was a standard building unit of about 13 ft.

sit back, drawing a large income simply by engaging a shepherd to look after a few hundred sheep. 'I thank my God', wrote one, 'And ever shall. It was the sheep that paid for all.[1] The prosperity of the yeoman accounts for a boom in domestic building that began in the middle of the sixteenth century and went on until the middle of the seventeenth. Most of England's many half-timber buildings (today referred to as cottages) date from this period.

Great attention was paid by those who could afford it to chimney stacks (hence in due course the tax on hearths), and in the 1570's, it is reported by William Harrison, elderly villagers would marvel and shake their heads to see 'the multitude of chimneys lately erected' where before even men of means were content to let the smoke escape through a hole in the roof of the hall or principal room. Harrison was an Essex parson who contributed to Holinshed's *Chronicle*. 'Never so much oke hath been spent in a hundred years before as in ten years of our time', he wrote in 1577, 'for everyman almost is a builder, and he that hath bought any small parcel of ground, be it ever so little, will not be quiet till he have pulled downe the old house, if anie were there standing, and set up a new after his own device.'

Harrison was wistful, even critical, of such amenities as bolsters in these new and improved dwellings. If men of his father's generation managed within seven years of marriage to buy a mattress and a sack of chaff for the head, they thought themselves as well lodged as the lord of the town. He himself had been wont to lay his head at night on a good round log. No record exists of Harrison's own house. It is known however, that village parsons, despite their background of education, were often little better off than the small farmers and petty freeholders; they cultivated the glebe and grazed the churchyard, yet lived in small cottages. At Medmenham, Buckinghamshire, the vicarage consisted, in 1605, of '2 baye built with mud walls and rough cast and covered with tyle, both bayes being chambered over and boarded, porched and a studdy over that'. In 1716 this cottage was rebuilt as two bays with flint and rubble.[2]

---

[1] Lines quoted by Hugh Braun in *Old English Houses*, 1962.
[2] A. H. Plaisted, *The Manor and Parish Records of Medmenham*, 1925, quoted by G. E. Fussell in *The English Rural Labourer*, 1949.

Cooking at a central hearth. Nineteenth-century print.

The burst of activity in putting up small houses for yeomen was accompanied by increased activity with mud and sticks by the poor as they added to wretched huddles of shacks on the village wastes. The golden fleeces which made the yeoman rich had reduced the need for farm labour. Many of the poor had no option but to become squatters. The miserable way of life of these unfortunate people made their hovels a nuisance which the parish authorities frowned on, in the way they often frown today on caravan camps. It was not uncommon for a hovel to be razed to the ground on the pretext that it harboured thieves.

In 1589 the Government took steps to check destitution, and Queen Elizabeth signed an Act against the Erecting and Maintaining of Cottages. This referred in its preamble to 'the great inconveniences which are found to grow by the creating . . . of great numbers and multitudes of cottages'. It was directed that in future no cottage was to be built unless four acres of land went with it. The land need not adjoin the cottage, but could be in strips in the common fields. In practice so many exceptions were allowed by the parish authorities that the Act caused only a partial check on hovel building. The justices in Quarter Sessions were often appealed to for help in disputes; indeed, much of the business of the Sessions had to do with ordering the pulling down of cottages or the granting of permission to erect them.

The Act of Settlement of 1662 indicates little change in the situation nearly a century later. This new measure sought to tie a man to the parish where he was born.

> By some defects of the law poor people are not restrained from going from one parish to another and therefore do endeavour to settle themselves in those parishes where there is the best stock, the largest commons or wastes to build cottages, and the most woods for them to burn and destroy; and when they have consumed it, then to another parish and at last become rogues and vagabonds . . .

In 1663 the Worcestershire Quarter Sessions sent out circular letters to the justices about 'the great number of cottages lately erected', acknowledging their care in this matter and reminding them it was 'a work of as great concernment as any we know, for the great neglect of late has been in this particular has caused this county to abound with poor more than any county we know of'.[1]

The wretched one-room hovel was to remain for several generations the most usual type of accommodation a traveller might see in a journey from Cornwall to Cumberland. The amenities of a typical example were described by John Taylor, the sailor-poet of James I's reign, when he was obliged to find somewhere to spend the night at Hastings:

> Within a cottage nigh, there dwells a weaver
> Who entertain'd as the like was never,
> No meat, no drink, no lodging (but the floor)
> No stool to sit, no lock upon the door,
> No straw to make us litter in the night,
> Nor any candlestick to hold the light.[2]

---

[1] Dorothy M. George.
[2] *A Discovery by Sea from London to Salisbury*, 1623.

An eighteenth-century cottager preparing fuel. George Morland.

It would not have occurred to Taylor to mention the absence of any kind of sanitary arrangement. Privies – sheds containing a bucket or some kind of opening in the ground – were a luxury for cottagers till far into the nineteenth century. Waste matter of all kinds was simply thrown outside. Given plenty of space, the results need not have been intolerable: E. Estyn Evans, writing in *Irish Folk Ways* (1957) of the humblest type of Irish farm, says that it is 'customary for women to use the byre and men the stable'.

The lavatory known since mediaeval times as a garderobe may be mentioned here: this was an upstairs closet with a stone or wooden seat over a chute, but it was confined to upper class and monastic houses. The building of garderobes practically ceased in the early seventeenth century in favour of the less spectacular close stool, a box with pierced seat that contained a pot. But it was rare indeed for the cottager to possess one in the seventeenth century.

3

Georgian Poverty

In the eighteenth century new methods of work were making agriculture and other industries more productive, and those who benefited, directly or indirectly, loved to build. The aristocracy and the newly rich employed architects to raise mansions; squires ordered gracious country houses with pillared Palladian porticos; lesser squires and business and professional men put up small Georgian residences in red brick or stone. Local builders now had access to the latest pattern books, and produced with ease the entirely regular-looking house which all clients wanted – a house with a symmetrically-placed front door and an equally symmetrical arrangement of sash windows. Timber-framed houses were out of fashion and often had new claddings in front to make them look Georgian. There was a craze, especially in the southeast, for an ingenious nail-hung tile which could make a timber-framed house appear a brick house.

The rural labourers of the eighteenth century lived in buildings that were by no means Georgian in appearance. The accommodation of the average mid-century cottage commonly consisted of one room only, though some of course had a lean-to shed, or outshut. In certain districts, cottage chimneys were still being built of poles daubed with clay. Furze was believed to be a good fuel and was widely collected from the common. Dried animals' dung was also used, where it could be spared.

Artificial light in the form of wax candles was rare except in the larger farmhouses; if the flames of the fire did not suffice for evening jobs, extra light would be provided by rushlights. The tedious procedure of dipping the rushes in grease has been described in Gilbert White's *Natural History of Selborne*. The still more tedious procedure, known to boy scouts, of getting the initial spark by means of a piece of steel, a flint and some tinder compels admiration.

In the earlier part of the eighteenth century many peasants nevertheless lived tolerably well compared with the peasants of other countries. Foreign visitors were surprised by the variety of their diet. Most cottagers had butcher's meat (costing about 3d a pound) once or twice a week, bacon from their own pigs, eggs from their own hens, and dark bread made of rye or bran. In the north of England less meat was eaten, but there was plenty of oatmeal, milk and cheese. All parts of the country enjoyed good

A mid-Georgian one-room cottage with unglazed windows. Engraving by J. T. Smith.

supplies of beer. St Bartholomew's Hospital allowed each patient over twenty pints a week, knowing it to be safer to drink than water.[1] Oliver Goldsmith's vicar of Wakefield offers this picture:

> The place of our retreat was in a little neighbourhood, consisting of farmers, who tilled their own grounds, and were equal strangers to opulence and poverty. As they had all the conveniences of life within themselves, they seldom visited towns and cities in search of superfluity. Remote from the polite, they still retained the primeval simplicity of manners; and frugal by habit, they scarce knew that temperance was a virtue. They wrought with cheerfulness on days of labour; but observed festivals as intervals of idleness and pleasure.

The vicar, with his wife and six children, had a cottage which 'consisted of but one storey, and was covered in thatch, which gave it an air of great snugness'.

By the 1740s the tenor of rural life was rapidly changing. The great enclosure operations had now begun in earnest – in George III's reign over three million acres were 'filched from the people' – and as one Enclosure Act followed another in the period 1740-1789 more and more peasants lost the measure of independence that came with owning small strips of land; they were bought out to make room for large compact estates with neatly hedged fields, cultivated by tenant farmers. Instead of living in the villages these farmers had new farmhouses out on the new holdings; sometimes there were unwanted manor houses suitable for them.

It was a good investment for an estate owner to build farmhouses (which today so handsomely decorate the English countryside), and a much less attractive one to build – or improve – cottages for the landless labourers. Existing cottages grew dilapidated, and were made the more uncomfortable to live in by the clutter connected with weaving, spinning, basket-making and other home crafts calculated to bring in a few extra shillings. A rising population – about $5\frac{1}{2}$ million in 1700 had become nearly 10 million by 1800 – led to dreadful overcrowding despite an appreciable drift to the towns; it also meant a glut of labour and wages far too low for a man to be able to spend anything on the improvement of his

---

[1] Warren Harvey in *Medical History*, January 1968.

'Equal strangers to opulence and poverty.' George Morland.

dwelling. 'Where plenty smiles,' wrote Crabbe in *The Village*, 'alas! She smiles for few.' Agricultural prosperity was paid for by a vast increase in rural poverty. The better roads and machines which diverted cottage industry to factories in towns, cut off cottagers, and especially their wives and children, from a source of income they had grown to rely on.

Between 1764 and 1775 a series of bad harvests forced up the price of necessities, creating a situation that was beneficial to the big farmers but crippling to the poor.[1] Then came the wars with France which made the cost of living rise so high that many families never had meat. There was no increase in wages. Sir Frederick Eden, writing of widespread wretchedness in his important study, *The State of the Poor* (1746), suggested that labourers make their wages more productive by means of 'a few little frugal arrangements at home'. He drew attention to the potato – 'this excellent root', he called it – and to soup making. 'There seems to be just reason to conclude that the miseries of the labouring Poor arise, less from the scantiness of their income (however much the philanthropists might wish it to be increased) than from their own improvidence and unthriftiness.' But poverty can be too deep for planned thriftiness. There is no reason to think that the farm labourers and their families described by William Cowper in *The Task* (1784), were unusual:

> They brave the season, and yet find at eve,
> Ill clad and fed but sparely, time to cool.
> The frugal housewife trembles when she lights
> Her scanty stock of brushwood, blazing clear,
> But dying soon, like all terrestial joys;
> The few small embers left she nurses well.
> And while her infants race with outstretched hands
> And crowded knees sit cowering o'er the sparks,
> Retires, content to quake, so they be warmed.
> The man feels least, as more inured than she
> To winter, and the current in his veins
> More briskly moved by his severer toil;
> Yet he too finds his own distress in theirs.
> The taper soon extinguished which I saw

---

[1]   See Oliver Goldsmith's *The Deserted Village*, 1769.

Rural housing in Middlesex. c. 1800. Engraving by J. T. Smith.

> Dangled along at the cold finger's end,
> Just when the day declined, and the brown loaf
> Lodged on the shelf, half eaten, without sauce
> Of savoury cheese, or butter costlier still,
> Sleep seems their only refuge; for alas!
> Where penury is felt the thought is chained,
> And sweet colloquial pleasures are but few. . . .

Landlords were often afraid that, if they built extra cottages or improved the old ones, the properties would eventually get lived in by people from other parishes who would become chargeable to the local poor rate – an annual sum paid by every householder. Under the Act of Settlement of 1662 anyone was eligible for some kind of relief from the parish where he had been born, or where he had achieved a settlement.

To the man who owned a whole parish, or several whole parishes, the poor rate was seen as a tiresome burden. Henry Fielding,[1] advocating regional houses of industry for the poor, considered that the money collected was illspent.

Proposal for Making an Effectual Provision for the Poor, 1751.

Every man, who hath any property, must feel the weight of that tax which is levied for the use of the Poor; and every man of any understanding must see how absurdly it is applied. . . . it is a question whether the Poor or the Rich are more dissatisfied, or have indeed greater reason to be dissatisfied; since the plunder of the one serves so little to the real advantage of the other; for while a million a year is raised among the former, many of the latter are starved; many more languish in want and misery; of the rest many more are found begging or pilfering . . .

A practical way for a landowner to keep down his liability for poor rate was to let cottages decay to the point of being unusable, or to find a pretext for actually pulling them down. By these measures potentially undesirable cottagers were forced to move to another parish or, if the parish officers there declined to help, to some area of waste land.

Elizabeth I's Act against erecting cottages unless four acres went with them – an Act long disregarded – was finally repealed in 1775. As Eden suggested, there no longer seemed any danger of cottages becoming too numerous:

I know of several parishes in which the greatest difficulty under which the Poor labour is the impossibility of procuring habitations. The present is said to be an age of speculation, and particularly so in building; but adventurers in this line, I believe, seldom think of erecting cottages in country parishes, on the contingent possibility of letting them to labourers' families. Neither can labourers themselves, who wish to migrate from their parents, and set up for themselves, although they may possess the small sum requisite to erect a cottage, always obtain permission from the lord of a manor to build one on a common.

Eden writes of poor people availing themselves of a long night to rear a hovel on the roadside or other piece of waste ground. Traditionally a squatter who could get a roof over his head without being caught making it had acquired a right to stay there, though on sufferance. After 60 years a freehold was established.

In *Remarks on Forest Scenery* (1791) William Gilpin complains of New Forest squatters who 'build their huts and inclose . . .

patches of ground without leave'. He tells of such dwellings being put up in a single night and residence demonstrated next morning by the kindling of a fire. Apparently between Beaulieu Manor and the Forest there was a large though scattered settlement of this kind. The ostensible business of the squatters was to cut furze for neighbouring lime kilns, but in Gilpin's opinion they were just poachers and timber thieves.

William Hutton, a poor stocking weaver who rose to be a bookseller, has left a record of an encounter with a family of squatters.[1] In the year 1750 he lost his way one night in crossing Charnwood Forest, five miles of uncultivated wasteland without any road. At last he came upon a cottage and induced its occupant to give him shelter. The cottager appeared strongly-built, but 'his manner was repelling as the rain and his appearance horrid as the night'. Next morning he was revealed as 'formed in one of Nature's coarsest moulds. His hands retained the accumulated filth of the last three months, garnished with half a dozen scabs; both perhaps, the result of idleness'. The wife, 'young, handsome, ragged and good-natured', three children and a gruesome aunt made up the household. There was no rushlight and no fire beyond 'a glow which would barely have roasted a potato'. The only food in the place was pease and water. For bedclothes Hutton was given a petticoat which the wife removed from her own bed.

---

[1] Quoted by Dorothy M. George.

4

Early Pattern Books

By the 1770s a few voices were beginning to be raised about the condition of the rural cottages and of those who lived in them; a few sensitive individuals were questioning, in pamphlets and books, the accepted view of the poor as a rabble of useful though near-insensate brutes. As a result there were landowners to whom it occurred, as they strolled about their estates, that the tiny shacks of their workers and their families, set at a distance from their own residences, were probably very inconvenient.

The notion was underlined in a well-written book of 1775, *Hints to Gentlemen of Landed Property* by Nathaniel Kent:

> The shattered hovels which half the poor of this kingdom are obliged to put up with, is truly affecting to a heart fraught with humanity. Those who condescend to visit these miserable tenements can testify that neither health or decency can be preserved in them.

Kent was a professional agriculturalist and land valuer and had visited many cottages. The weather, he said, frequently penetrated all parts of them, causing every kind of illness and early shaking the constitutions of children. It was shocking that a man, his wife and half a dozen children should be obliged to sleep in one room together, and even more shocking that the wife should have no private place to be brought to bed in. Gentlemen of landed property bestowed considerable attention on their stables and kennels, but were apt to look on cottages as incumbrances and clogs, whereas those who occupied them were the very nerves and sinews of agriculture. Estates with even the richest soil were of no value without hands to cultivate them. 'Nay', he declared, 'I will be

A hovel in Chelsea c. 1800. Engraving by J. T. Smith.

bold to aver, that more real advantages flow from cottages, than from any other source; for besides their great utility to landed property, they are the greatest support to the state, as being the most prolific cradles of population.'

Kent's book was the first to contain plans for model cottages. Of these he observed that there was, of course, no point in labourers' dwellings being fine or expensive:

All that is requisite is a warm, comfortable, plain room for the poor inhabitants to eat their morsel in, an oven to bake their bread, a little receptacle for their small beer and provisions and two wholesome lodging apartments, one for the man and his wife and another for his children. It would perhaps be more decent if the boys and girls could be separated, but this would make the building too expensive and besides is not so materially necessary; for the boys find employment in farmhouses at an early age.

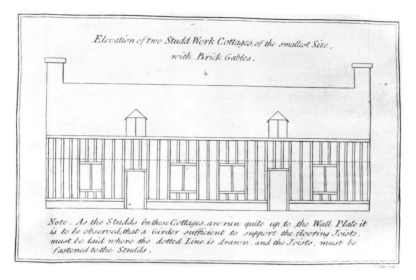

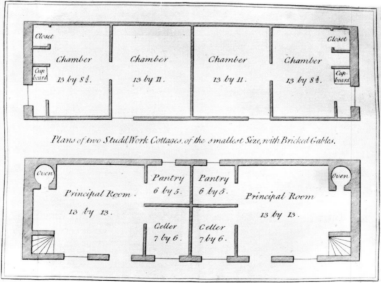

Model pair with stud frame. From Nathaniel Kent's Hints to Gentlemen of Landed Property, *1775.*

Kent estimated that a two-bedroomed cottage of brick should cost £66 and of wood, £58. Lord Brownlow and several other landowners are reported to have carried out work according to his directions.

Compared with the rent-producing farmhouses, cottages, it should be repeated, were a poor investment; but moral blackmail was beginning to operate and various squires, themselves living in luxury and ease, deliberately set out to rival each other in the benevolence and liberality of their building operations. Designs for cottages began to appear in architectural pattern books where previously nothing lower than a large farmhouse had been discussed. There was emerging what is now considered the true labourer's cottage, something built by a professional builder who followed a drawing.

England's first architectural book devoted *entirely* to cottages was John Wood's *Series of Plans for Cottages or Habitations of the Labourer*, 1781. Wood, who designed the Royal Crescent and other terraces in Bath, states in the introduction that his book sprang from a conversation about rural dwellings with a group of gentlemen landowners. These, much to their credit, seem to have become distressed by 'the indecent and inhuman conditions' of the cottages on their estates. Before producing his designs, Wood went to look at a number of cottages near Bath. 'The greater part of those that fell within my observation', he writes, 'I found to be shattered, dirty, inconvenient, miserable hovels, scarcely affording a shelter for the beasts of the forest, much less were they proper habitations for the human species. . . .' Often he found a man and his wife and some half-dozen children crowding together at night in the same bed; like Kent, he was humane in a way not typical of the eighteenth century.

He even insisted in his proposals that every cottage should have a privy (that is, instead of nothing at all except a pot): 'This convenience should answer many good ends, but in nothing more than being an introduction to cleanliness'. Even in farmhouses privies were rare at this date. Wood writes of villages and towns 'where there is scarcely such a convenience in the whole place, for want of which the streets are perfect jakes . . .' A village street is described by Crabbe as follows:

> Between the road way and the walls, offense,
> Invades all eyes and strikes on every sense;

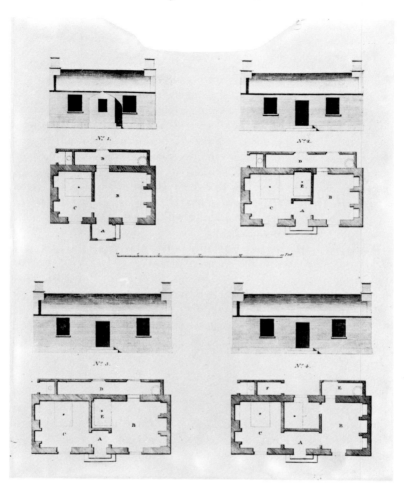

Two-room cottages. From John Wood's Plans for Cottages, *1781*.

There lie, obscene, at every open door,
Heaps from the hearth and sweeping from the floor,
And day by day the mingled masses grow. . . .

Wood's designs and remarks were strictly practical. He makes the point that if cottages are built in pairs 'the inhabitants may be of assistance to each other in case of sickness or any other accident'. An idea still lingered in the country that the south wind brought the plague, and principal windows therefore faced north. But Wood said: 'Let the window of the main room receive its light from the East or the South; then it will always be warm and cheerful'. He adds this: 'So like the feelings of men in an higher sphere are those of the poor cottager, that if his habitation be warm, cheerful and comfortable, he will return to it with gladness, and abide in it with pleasure'.

Wood is insistent about only one aesthetic requirement, regularity – which in his view is beauty. The importance he attaches to regularity is shown by his addition of blind windows and doors to give an axial and symmetrical facade without imposing on the convenience of the plan. It was a long time before Wood's designs for small cottages were bettered; they were found of practical use by individuals as well as by his landowner patrons.

5

Cult of the Picturesque

To some landlords in the second half of the eighteenth century, cottage building was attractive only if it could be seen as an artistic exercise according to picturesque principles. It was becoming the fashion to redesign estates and gardens to make them look like the landscapes admired in contemporary paintings: lakes were formed, hills moved and fake ruins constructed. William Kent, in designing part of Kensington Gardens, actually planted dead trees to increase the similarity of a view to a picture by Salvator Rosa. A few squires, Charles Hamilton of Pains Hill for one, employed a hermit to live picturesquely in a thatched hermitage in the woods. The duties of such a hermit were set out in Richard Graves's *Columella* (1779): 'to keep his hermitage clean and to sit at the door with a book in his hand when any company came'.

The old cottages, cramped, insanitary and ruinous, tended to be picturesque already. But where a landlord made up his mind to build new ones, it might amuse him to adopt the picturesque style of architecture. From the 1780s designs for picturesque cottages appeared constantly in the pattern books published by architects. These cottages were not regular in the plain style of Wood; the concern of their designers was for the charms of ruggedness and rusticity.

James Malton was the first to isolate the picturesque as a quality in architecture which, by taking thought, can be created. His *Essay on British Cottage Architecture* (1798) was meant to guide builders on how best to preserve the vernacular, 'to perpetuate on Principle that Peculiar mode of building which was originally the effect of chance'; his book was also calculated to persuade gentlemen clients that Malton cottages would make very pleasant

Hermitage for a gentleman's park. From Le Rouge's Jardins Anglo-Chinois, *1776.*

Picturesque cottages. From James Malton's Essay on British Cottage Architecture, *1798.*

retreats, not only for their hedgers and ditchers, but for themselves. Taking as his starting point the popular notion about the tranquil and innocent life of the rustic peasant, Malton looked at existing old cottages, noted the effects of 'time, weather and chance', then set out principles by which the picturesque might be attained. Above all, the cottage must be irregular. The walls were to be of unequal height; projecting parts such as eaves gables, porches, and latticed windows were to be bold enough to produce a 'judicious contrast of light and shade'; the colour and texture of the building were to be varied in such a way that they suggested the effect of accident. Today Malton's three-roomed dwellings would produce a crisis if submitted to any planning authority.

David Laing set out to create the 'painter-like' effects recommended by Sir Uvedale Price, whose *Essays on the Picturesque* (1794), concerning *banditti*, ruins and shaggy donkeys, did much to establish the cult. Laing's cottages and farmhouses – in his elegantly engraved *Hints for Dwellings* (1801) – were picturesque in their eccentricity and in the way in which several had been designed 'for particular Situations in which the Peculiarities of the surrounding Scenery have been attended to'. One of his favourite cottage plans was an octagon with a pair of wings forming an angle of about 120 degrees on the front. But however irregular the plans, the elevations have a Grecian regularity. Laing was the architect of the London Custom House in Lower Thames Street (1813-17): his career ended in disgrace in 1825 when the centre of this building sank on its foundations and had to be rebuilt at great expense.

Richard Elsam was against genteel imitations of old and miserable dwellings, but he was not against improving them. He chose an appropriate time, 1816, for offering to the world a book called *Hints for Improving the Condition of the Peasantry*. The previous year peace with France had been restored by the Treaty of Paris and most sections of the ruling class, among whom fears of an English version of the French Revolution were never entirely absent, wished to appear concerned about the comfort, health and morals of the poor. The book was dedicated to one of the greatest improvers of agricultural buildings, Thomas Coke of Holkham, Norfolk.

Elsam's designs were intended to introduce a simple, though

A cottage 'to correspond with its situation'. From David Laing's Hints for Dwellings, *1801.*

not rude, style that gave the impression of having been conceived by the cottagers themselves. He defended symmetry for buildings of any consequence, but said that for rural cottages irregularity was essential. It was of first importance, too, to choose a picturesque site, for landscape was the only thing that could make such buildings 'objects of interest and admiration'; but unlike Laing he stipulated settling the plan first, the site second. To illustrate the effect of landscaping Elsam provided a scenic elevation as well as two perspective views of each design.

The famous architect Sir John Soane contrived to combine rustic associations with regularity in the Grecian mode: outside and inside were symmetrical. There are seven designs for labourers' cottages in his *Sketches in Architecture* (1798).

Among the more notable examples of work done according to such drawings are the thatched village of Blaise, near Bath, laid out by John Nash; Nuneham Courtney, Oxfordshire, with its double

A design for an octagonal cottage with wings. From Laing's Hints for Dwellings, *1801.*

row of cottages in brick and timber; and Milton Abbas, Dorset, built in one operation to replace a village demolished because it did not accord with the peaceful landscaping of the squire's estate.

Picturesque cottages were often not without certain disadvantages to those who had to live in them. Christopher Holdenby wrote in *Folk of the Furrow* (1913) of the kind with artistically sloping roofs and exiguous windows.

> When one has no choice of bedrooms, gables and eaves are often a picturesque cruelty by every inch of height and light and air of which they deprive human beings. . . . As every inch of space is reduced, these details become more insupportable – windows never made to open, or, in tiny rooms, occupying the only wall space where a bed can be placed.

But the cottage builders who bothered to be deliberately picturesque were a minority; most stuck to basic practicalities. In the matter of floors, for example, smart pattern books might call for certain types of stone or tile, but one could always follow John Mordant, author of *The Compleat Steward* (1761), who said that earth floors were perfectly all right. Such floors were made of one-third lime, one-third coal ashes well sifted and one-third loamy clay and horse dung made from grass, these last two in equal proportions. Another sort could be made of loamy clay with one-third new soft horse dung with a small quantity of coal ashes. The material was tempered, rested for ten days, again tempered and rested for three days, then laid upon the ground. Making floors like this was a well-established practice; they were known as lime-ash floors. As late as 1831 Thomas Postans proposed cottages with walls made of clay and straw, and roofs of poles and thatch; the accommodation was to consist of a living room and two bedrooms – all on the ground floor.

6

The Regency Poor

Widespread unemployment came with the ending of the French wars in 1815; and returning soldiers and sailors added another half million to the workless. For a time there was a fever of cottage building, though a disregard for the convenience of working-class families is obvious from a look at the printed designs of the period. In *The Rural Architect* Joseph Gandy illustrated a £90 gardener's cottage which contained two rooms seven feet high – a kitchen 9 ft 9 in by 14 ft and one bedroom 9 ft 9 in by 8 ft. A double cottage for a general labourer contained a kitchen 10 ft 3 in by 13 ft, a workroom 13 ft by 16 ft and a bedroom 8 ft by 16 ft.

But for the poor, merely to have a sound roof constituted a blessing. William Howitt, who undertook excursionary sharings in the lives of the common people in the 1820s (as did George Borrow), gives this description of 'cottage life in its best estate, in its unsophisticated and unpauperized condition':[1]

> When we go into the cottage of the working man . . . there is his tenement of, at most, one or two rooms. His naked walls; bare brick stone or mud floor, as it may be; a few wooden or rush-bottomed chairs; a deal or old oak table; a simple fire place, a few pots and pans – and you have his whole abode, goods and chattels. He comes home weary from his out-door work, and seats himself for a few hours with his wife and children, then turns into a rude bed, standing perhaps on the farther side of his only room. Sundays, and a few holidays, are white days in his calendar. On them he shaves and puts on a clean shirt and better coat drawn from

[1] *Rural Life of England*, 1838.

35

A Regency landlord visiting tenantry, 1810. George Cruickshank.

the old chest which contains the whole wardrobe . . . Then
he walks round his little garden, if he have it; goes with his
wife and children to church or meeting; to sit with a
neighbour, or have a neighbour look in upon him.

Existing cottages were generally worst in the North and in Scotland;
though Howitt's tiny hovel-workshops of Yorkshire and Lanca-
shire, crowded to the walls with offspring, could be matched in
most parts of the South.

Up to the 1820s the peasantry of the Sutherland estates were
living in conditions reminiscent of the Dark Ages, according to an
account by James Loch, a Member of Parliament. Their huts, he
said, dipped down with the slope of the ground; they were built
of turf dug from the most valuable parts of the mountain sides and
roofed with turves supported on branches of trees. The inhabitants
shared a roof with pigs and poultry and used the same door. The
fire was set in the middle of the earth floor and its smoke allowed to
circulate throughout the hut for the purpose of conveying heat.
'The effect was to cover everything with a black glossy soot, and
to produce the most evident injury to the appearance and eyesight

of those most exposed to its influence.' Loch is quoted in George Smith's *Essay on the Construction of Cottages* (1834), which observes that in cottages of only one room 'the young people must contract indelicate habits unfavourable to their good conduct in after life'.

A Board of Agriculture survey of cottages,[1] prepared at the close of the eighteenth century, gives some idea of distribution. The typical cottage, it disclosed, had but a single bedroom of the hayloft type, whatever the materials of its construction. Dorset was still rich in cottages made of road scrapings; and on the outskirts of wastes in Surrey and Hampshire there were plenty of turf huts occupied by squatters. The situation had changed little, apparently, from that at the beginning of the century. Mud cottages were common in most parts of the country, though the most usual material for new building was now stone, brick or half-timber. Windows were glazed, though not necessarily made to open. The Home Counties were the best-housed because the builders were influenced by modern practice in London – though in Hertfordshire there was much walling of laths daubed with crumbling clay and lime. The typical cottage south of the Thames was a more substantial structure of brick or half-timber, even if it had only one bedroom. Kent was well off for cottages of sound studwork faced with tiles, and for brick ones; however, mud cottages existed there, too. In Buckinghamshire new cottages were being built of brick, or of mud and timber quarterings. Those in the open-field parishes were very bad. Essex had a large quota of clay-daubed cottages ill repaired and thatched. In the neighbourhood of Colchester, then a more important centre than today, ornamental treatment of exterior plaster was found to flourish.

More efficient methods of farming had been introduced in parts of Norfolk and Suffolk, but these counties were fortunate in their cottages only where the great improvers had been at work. Sir Robert Walpole, in the early years of the eighteenth century, had made Houghton a neat village of brick buildings, uniform inside and out, with rents at a guinea a year. Thomas Coke, the agricultural reformer, had built some good three-bedroom cottages at Holkham, some in groups of four backing on to one another.

[1] Analysed by G. E. Fussell.

The sleeping loft in a Yorkshire cottage. A drawing by Sydney R. Jones in Old English Household Life *by Gertrude Jekyll and Sydney R. Jones, 1925.*

L. Simond, a French visitor, wrote in 1815 of seeing large farm-houses and substantial outbuildings in Norfolk and Suffolk, but so few cottages that he asked himself where or how the common labourers could live (a lot of them would have been crowded into redundant farmhouses in the villages). The Suffolk cottages seemed very poor, but he noted casements in good repair and clean floors.

To the south-west, cottages became steadily worse through Hampshire, Berkshire, Wiltshire and Dorset, especially where the farms were large. Earth walls built with a dung fork were common in Wiltshire, though between Stourhead and Sherborne sandstone walls provided dry quarters. In Berkshire numerous cottages had broken windows, leaky thatch and earth floors.

The mud or cob cottages of Devon (well-tended survivals today attract tourists) were said to have an air of squalor and meanness and to be universally condemned. The fact is, without good thatch and foundations, cob soon disintegrates with the action of rain; and many Devon cottages were so poorly looked after as to be unsafe. There is a report of a midsummer rainstorm which demolished twenty; the rain was so heavy that the walls of clay and chopped straw collapsed within hours. One old lady was drowned in her bed.

At Tiverton cottages of red brick and stone mingled with those of cob. Over the previous half century sixty-four cottages here had become complete ruins – partly, it seems, because of the decline of the woollen industry and partly as a result of enclosures. In Cornwall, too, numerous cottages had fallen into utter decay, largely because of the fragility of the building materials. Although stone was more plentiful than in Devon, cob was a usual Cornish building material. Holdings were extremely small and farmhouse and cottage were barely distinguishable; some farmhouses had no more than a single bedroom. Whole villages, like Sennen near Land's End, were built of mud, but a few stone and slate farm houses were going up around 1800.

In Somerset the cottagers were little better off. The whole of the more remote of the south-western counties were poorly housed, with the exception of those farmers who occupied old manor houses or new buildings on large holdings. West of Dorset there were few such buildings.

In Cambridgeshire and Lincolnshire cottage building had by no means kept pace with farming improvements. Both farmhouses and one-up-and-one-down cottages were of stud and mud, or lath and plaster. Conditions were similar in Bedfordshire, though on the Duke of Bedford's estate cottages of two, three and four bedrooms had been built. Inferior cottages were usual in Leicestershire, Northamptonshire and Warwickshire. There were a few stone cottages in Northamptonshire: the fact that nearly all were found to be in villages is an indication of their pre-enclosure origin.

Cottages in Yorkshire were often of stone, but they were thinly spread and labourers – most of them unmarried – boarded in the farmhouses. Housing in the East and North Ridings was worse than in the West. The North Riding cottages were stated to have one room only.

One-room stone cottages were common in Durham, Northumberland, Cumberland and Westmorland. John Bailey, who wrote

A good type of cottage kitchen. Note the pot hung over an open fire, and the capacity for three-legged tables to stand firm on uneven floors. George Morland.

Interior of an eighteenth-century weaver's cottage with central hearth. Contemporary print.

a book about the agriculture of Durham in 1810, dismissed the cottages as 'in general comfortable dwellings of one storey, thatched or tiled, and much the same as those in other districts'. Like many of his contemporaries, he did not consider the housing of labourers a matter of much importance.

Northumberland was a district of thatched roofs. The rural cottages were of mediaeval standards, especially near the Borders. William Hutchinson, author of several contemporary travel books, wrote of them thus:

The cottages of the lower class of people are deplorable, composed of upright timbers fixed in the ground, the interstices wattled and plastered with mud; the roofs, some thatched and others covered with turf; one little piece of glass to admit the beams of day; and a hearthstone on the ground, for the peat and turf fire. Within there was exhibited a scene to touch the feelings of the heart; description sickens on the subject . . . the damp earth, the naked rafters, the breeze-disturbed embers, and distracted smoke that issued from the hearth . . . the midday gloom, the wretched couch, the wooden utensils that scarce retain the name of convenience, the domestic beast that stalls with his master, the disconsolate poultry that mourns upon the rafters, form a group of objects suitable for a great man's contemplation.

Only in the vales along the Tyne was bare-footed poverty absent in a district of gentlemen's seats and well-built farmhouses.

If all this is a fair general summary of what rural cottagers had to live in, it may be wondered how any could live happily. But domestic happiness was indeed enjoyed, unobtrusively, even by some of the poorest. To people who had accepted poverty as their unalterable lot, quite small achievements like full dinner plates or a good fire on a cold evening were joys that went a long way to make up for conditions the well-off would think intolerable. Nor, of course, was it always winter. There were long months in which the deep mud was no more and when children might have the whole of the neighbouring countryside for a playground; they learned young to avoid such perils as eating the wrong berries and falling into water that was out of their depth.

For parents family life must often have seemed too much and too near; but there it was, offering relief in affliction, interest and occasionally hope. William Howitt could write as a serious student of English cottage life: 'I often thank God that the poor have their objects of admiration and attraction; their domestic affections and their family ties, out of which spring a thousand simple and substantial pleasures; that beauty and ability are not the exclusive growth of hall and palace . . .' He observed the 'sweet faces and lovely forms' to be seen 'by the evening passer-by in the light of the ingle, amid the family group, making some smoky-raftered hut a little temple of rare beauty.'

Crabbe, who had seen the poor at their most miserable, expressed a similar thought:

> There are who labour through the year, and yet
> No more have gained than – not to be in debt;
> Who still maintain the same laborious course,
> Yet pleasure hails them from some favourite source;

And health, amusement, children, wife, or friend,
With life's dull views their consolations blend.

To be a happy cottager it was necessary to be robust in mind and body. Many of the country people *were* robust at this period; they had just enough food of a kind to keep them going and unlimited fresh air and exercise to toughen them. Women there were with the spirit and energy not only to scrub their floors but also to whitewash the inside of the least promising cabins.

Cottagers with small gardens often took full advantage of them. Outdoor work with hoe and spade, which may have started as a means of bringing more food to the table, sometimes turned into a permanent and absorbing hobby. The practice of a fireside craft could give both men and women a sense of achievement and something to look forward to next day. It may have been unusual, but there existed poverty-stricken cottagers who had become absorbed by the study of some branch of natural history. Crabbe writes:

> Oft have I smiled the happy pride to see
> Of humble tradesmen in their evening glee;
> When of some pleasing, fancied good possessed,
> Each grew alert, was busy, and was blest.

7

The Victorian Poor

J. C. Loudon's *Encyclopaedia of Cottage, Farm and Villa Architecture*, which became a standard reference work for cottage builders in the nineteenth century, was hailed on its publication in 1833 with surprised admiration by both architects and reformers. Loudon himself was a landscape gardener rather than a trained architect. His work contained eighty-one designs for cottages and for furniture to go inside them. A rich blend of romanticism, practical advice and comment, it is a landmark in the history of cottages.

Loudon timed it well, for the dilapidation of rural property – resulting from the agricultural depression – and the state of the poor in general were becoming a noticeable scandal. 'Look at these hovels, made of mud and straw, bits of glass or of old cast-off windows, without frames or hinges frequently. Enter them and look at the bits of chairs and stools, the wretched boards tacked together to form a table . . .' So wrote Cobbett in *Rural Rides* after riding through Leicestershire.

Another traveller described some of the hinds' cottages in Northumberland and noted that they are 'much more comfortable than labourers' cottages often are':

> They are of one storey and generally of one room. On one side is the fireplace, with an oven on one hand and a boiler on the other; on the opposite side of the cottage is the great partition for the beds, which are two in number, with sliding doors or curtains. The ceiling is formed by poles nailed across from one side of the roof to the other, about half a yard from where it begins to slope, and covered with matting.

Labourers were becoming increasingly demoralized as well as increasingly poor. As for sexual morality, sleeping arrangements gave little chance for this to develop, particularly on the large estates of Durham and Northumberland where it was a condition of a hind's tenancy of his cottage that he provide and house a female labourer. James Cunningham wrote of Border peasants in 1842: 'Before we can hope to see them chaste, pure or elevated in morals, we must provide them with houses in which propriety and common decency may be observed'.

Since the latter part of the eighteenth century, few farm workers had been able to support a family on wages of a few shillings a week – wages which a laissez-faire government had no intention of raising, preferring a system of supplements from the poor rate. For forty years, following an Act of 1795 which sanctioned relief at home, the rates grew heavier each year; some men gloomily prophesied that they would eventually absorb the entire rent of the kingdom. Thus the Poor Law, designed to relieve the necessities of the poor, had become their bondage. The difference between the wage a labourer's master was prepared to give and the recognized minimum was made up by the parish; labourers who could not find private employment were either shared out among the ratepayers or had their labour sold by the parish to employers at a low rate, the parish contributing what was needed to bring wages up to scale. Refused a minimum wage and allotments, the labourers were given instead what amounted to a system of pauperism.[1]

In *The Annals of the British Peasantry* (1895) Russell M. Garnier wrote that whole administrative centres became convict colonies. 'Family by family, the entire labouring population would degenerate into paupers, bound to toil but doing it with marked reluctance. All fared alike, whether industrious or idle.'

The scale allowance arrangement included children, whose parents could draw so many loaves (or their equivalent) for each child. It was the one bright spot in the system that no one was omitted; no enquiry was made into the state of wedlock of the parents, and many single women drew allowances for one, two and three children.[2] A Swaffham, Norfolk, woman, with five

[1] J. L. and Barbara Hammond, *The Village Labourer*, 1911.
[2] G. E. Fussell.

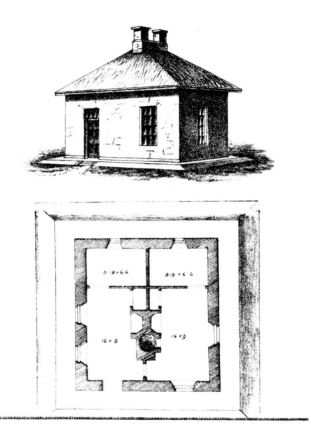

A cottage in J. C. Loudon's Encyclopaedia of Cottage, Farm and Villa Architecture, *1833. Loudon describes it as suitable for 'a working mechanic, a shoemaker or weaver' who is 'supposed to have a wife but no children'. The front room on the left is for his work, while the other front room is the kitchen. One of the two small bedrooms (9 ft 9 in by 6 ft 6 in) is recommended for stores.*

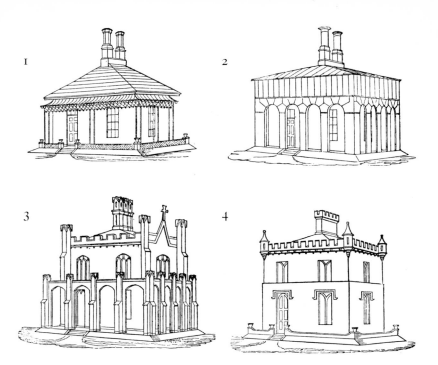

Five sketches show how the cottage opposite might be dressed up 'to display architectural style'. The ground floor plan is unaltered. 1. A verandah, a terrace parapet and chimney pots are added. 2. The roof is disguised with a second, false, roof supported on a screen front of light trellis work. Loudon recommends covering both screen and roof with vegetation, and draws the attention of the industrious cottager to apple and pear trees. 3. Another storey is added and the cottage becomes castellated Gothic. 4. Monastic Gothic. 5. Elizabethan.

'It may appear improbable to some', says Loudon, 'that a person purposing to build so small a dwelling, should think of applying any of these styles to it; but, in particular situations in Britain, it is sometimes considered desirable to render such dwellings striking objects in a view.'

I

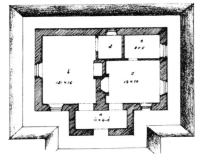

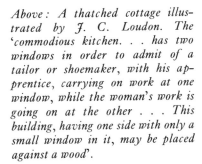

2

Above: A thatched cottage illustrated by J. C. Loudon. The 'commodious kitchen. . . has two windows in order to admit of a tailor or shoemaker, with his apprentice, carrying on work at one window, while the woman's work is going on at the other . . . This building, having one side with only a small window in it, may be placed against a wood'.

3

Right above: Three ideas for variation. Loudon considers that the dignity arising from tall windows is 'sadly counteracted by the mean, crouching appearance of the thatched roof'. 1. truncated gable ends have disappeared and the surface of the roof has been increased. Loudon comments: 'Proportion is restored, the eye is satisfied and the expression of a thatched cottage comparatively complete'. 2. The cottage has achieved a 'highly architectural character'. It was recommended in this guise for the suburbs of a village. 3. Gothic style, with battlements.

48

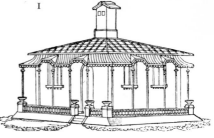

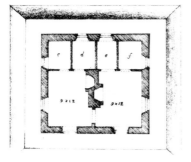

Above: A cottage illustrated by J. C. Loudon and criticized by him for its squat chimney stack rising from the roof without preparation.

Right above: Two ideas for variation. 1. Italian style. A verandah and an Italian parapet have been added, and the chimney stack has become imposing. 2. A style which Loudon describes as Indian Gothic.

illegitimate children to support, drew 18s a week: this was much more than any individual labourer could earn.[1] The cost of pauperism per head in 1832 was about 15s a year. It is not to be wondered at that the landlords on whom it fell were not enthusiastic about building new cottages.

In 1834 the situation of the poor was changed abruptly with the passing of the new Poor Law. Under this, outdoor relief was abolished and the workhouse test imposed on all applicants for public alms. 'An operation was necessary to save society', writes G. M. Trevelyan in *English Social History* (1944), 'but the knife

[1] Lord Ernle, *English Farming Past and Present.*

was applied without anaesthetics'. To encourage the labouring classes somehow to fend for themselves, conditions in the workhouses were made even more unpleasant than they had been before.

The new Poor Law did, however, inaugurate a more productive state of affairs. The attitude of the farmers seemed to change overnight. G. E. Fussell writes: 'At any time in the previous twenty years they would have declared that they could not provide full employment, at any rate if they had to pay all the necessary weekly wages for all the available labour, but almost immediately the Act forbidding outdoor relief had been passed they began to absorb it'. As little as three years after the passing of the Act, in 1837 (the year of Queen Victoria's accession), a Sussex farmer told a Commons Committee that some thirty or forty local men who had been provided for, and even paid without doing a hand's turn, had nearly all found employment in the parish. A Lords Committee was told that, in Hampshire, the unemployed had all been absorbed locally; and that, in fact, more men would have been found useful. Other counties were less fortunate, and children who had drawn the bread allowance now had to go to work on the farms to help close the gap between wages and the cost of living.

It was becoming clear that farming had begun to recover from the post-war depression. The comparative prosperity for landlords and farmers of the years 1840-70 is reflected in the number of cottages dating from this period. The Royal Agricultural Society of England, formed in 1839, took a theoretical interest in the condition of the labourer, and published in its journal articles and plans to do with cottages. The Duke of Bedford wrote proudly of those he had been building on his Bedfordshire and Devon estates, and observed that while other landlords were building and improving cattle sheds they should also build and improve dwellings for their labourers.

Plenty of farms existed where the cattle were indeed more attractively housed than those who had charge of them. James Cunningham, a Berwickshire surveyor, reported in 1842 that the workers' cottages were very often the worst in a steading. 'The barns and stables, for instance, are always finished more carefully; in these the walls are plastered, the roof and wood-work close and complete, and the floors either boarded or carefully paved . . .' But gradually some of the worst hovels were cleared away. As a

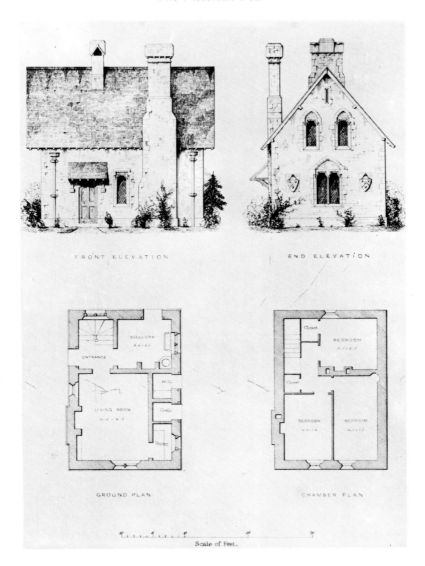

A prosperous version of the 'old English' style. From John Vincent's Country Cottages, *1861*.

Improved farm cottages built in 1848, with a sample of those they replaced.
From William Gray's Rural Architecture, *1852.*

source of practical advice on what to build in their place, John
Morton's *Cyclopaedia of Agriculture* (1856) took its place beside
Loudon's *Encyclopaedia of Cottage, Farm and Villa Architecture.*

Both Morton and Loudon put up a good case for a primitive
type of water closet and for the use of sewage in vegetable growing.
Loudon said that no cottage was complete, in his eyes,

> without this appendage [the w.c.] under the same roof, or
> under a lean-to. The well or tanks for liquid manure con-
> nected with it, are as advantageous, in point of profit, to every
> cottager who has a garden, as the water closet or privy itself
> is essential to cleanliness and decency.

Few people paid any attention to this idea.

Water closets, which had begun to be installed in some of the
big houses late in the eighteenth century, were still novelties;
and to work properly they needed careful maintenance. Landlords
excused themselves for not attempting the costly innovation for
cottages on the ground that cesspool contents would never be
cleared, let alone used in a controlled way as manure. Tenants
were left to make their own, usually casual, arrangements.

Even earth closets were not installed as a matter of course in new
cottages until the latter part of the nineteenth century. There is an

account of two farmers noting with surprise, as they rode by, that a landlord was having earth closets added to some Dorset cottages. One remarked; 'I tell you what it is, James, they will be giving them horses to ride to work on next'.[1] It is relevant to add that the sanitary authorities of those days, the boards of guardians, tended also to be big property owners.

After 1875 the building and repairing of cottages was undertaken with reluctance: an influx of cheap grain from America had brought about a sudden and prolonged collapse in English agriculture. When cottages had to be built, absurd economies might be made in wall thickness and in materials used as mortar. After the year 1879, in which all crops failed and livestock died in thousands, farm buildings and cottages virtually ceased to be rebuilt, or even maintained. For twenty years or more there was no general prosperity in the farming industry.

There have been many evocations of life in this later period of depression. The author with the pseudonym Miss Read writes of a characteristic situation in *Miss Clare Remembers* (1962):

> Esther was a tall thin child . . . she looked perpetually frightened, as no doubt she was. Her father was a heavy drinker and violent in his cup. He was a ploughman, but at that time when so much arable land was being turned over to pasture, he had been put to sheep-minding, hedging and ditching, mucking out stalls and cowsheds, and other jobs which he considered beneath him. Had he realized it, he was fortunate to have been kept in work at all by his hard-pressed employer.

R. E. Moreau writes of an Oxfordshire cottager with nine children being driven to suicide by his poverty, and remarks that an occupier of this cottage in the 1960s had a Jaguar.

By the end of the century the corn area in England and Wales had shrunk, according to Trevelyan, from over eight million acres in 1871 to under six million. Permanent pasture had greatly increased, but the introduction of frozen meat from abroad in the late eighties had caused cattle and sheep prices to match the fall in the price of corn. Farm workers were flocking to the towns. Lord Ernle writes in *English Farming*:

[1] Llewellyn Powis, *Dorset Essays*, 1935.

Economies of the 1870s. Dust from the roads and the contents of ash pits are ground up with 'a bare pretence of lime' to make mortar and plaster. Fires are lit against the thin, propped walls to encourage the mortar to set. Drawn by Dr T. Pridgin Teale in his book Dangers to Health, *1878.*

Thrown on their own resources, agriculturalists fought the unequal contest with courage and tenacity. But as time went on, the stress told more and more heavily. Manufacturing populations seemed to seek food-markets everywhere except at home. Enterprise gradually weakened; landlords lost their ability to help, farmers their recuperative power.... Prolonged depression checked costly improvements. Drainage was practically discontinued. Both owners and occupiers were engaged in the task of making both ends meet on vanishing incomes.

Even so, there were plenty of wage-earning cottagers in England whose spirit was far from crushed. In *Lark Rise* (1939) Flora Thompson describes in detail how it was possible for a farm labourer's family in a Northamptonshire hamlet to keep well afloat in the 1880s on the man's standard wage of half a guinea a week; wives even had something in hand to offer the more hungry of the tramps who begged at doors. 'In spite of their poverty and the worry and anxiety attending it, they were not unhappy, and though poor, there was nothing sordid about their lives.'

'The cottages were kept clean by much scrubbing with soap and water and doors and windows stood open when weather permitted. Though food was rough and teeth neglected, indigestion was unknown, while nervous troubles ... had yet to be invented.' Every family kept a pig in a lean-to shed beside or at the back of the cottage, and the pig became almost a member of the family: even so, it was rare for anyone to lose his appetite for sentimental reasons on the occasion of the annual feast of pork. The gardens were fully used for vegetables and herbs and as a site for rows of beehives, while the hedgerows were plucked of ingredients for wines and jellies.

Most of the cottages, said Flora Thompson, had one room only downstairs. In some the furniture was just a table, a few chairs and stools and a potato sack for a hearthrug, but others contained 'dressers of crockery, cushioned chairs, pictures on the walls and brightly coloured handmade rugs on the floor. In these there would be pots of geraniums, fuchsias and old fashioned, sweet-smelling musk on the window sills.'

8

Beginnings of Rural Public Health

Despite the exodus of country people to the towns, there was no sign, at the start of the twentieth century, that cottage accommodation was becoming more plentiful. In general terms, it was satisfactory only on big estates with a resident landlord or a good agent. In a letter to *The Times* in 1898 the chairman of a parish council wrote as follows:

> In very many districts the farmers and others cannot get enough men to do their work because there are no houses for them. And not only are cottages scarce, but in many country villages they are in a wretched state of neglect and overcrowding, whole families being still reared in the single bedroom. . . .

The explanation was simply that cottage building had not kept pace during the hard times with the number of cottages which had disintegrated. But at least the practice of pulling down houses to avoid poor rates ceased when parishes were amalgamated into unions by the Union Chargeability Act.

A book called *English Country Cottages* (1900) by J. L. Green, a sanitary inspector, makes it clear that eighteenth-century conditions were still everywhere to be met. In numerous cottages with which Green was acquainted, the kitchen-cum-livingroom was so small that an ordinary family could scarcely turn around in it.

> At meal times it is quite impossible for all to sit down together at a table. They must have their meals in twos and threes at the table, or must sit in any odd corner, holding

The family gathered in a typically cramped kitchen-cum-living room. A late eighteenth-century engraving by Stephen Miller.

their cups or plates on their laps. There is no arrangement downstairs for washing the clothes, such as a copper. . . . On family washing days the wife of the breadwinner boils her water in small pots over her front room fire, takes it to the back, pours it into the washing-tub or other receptacle, and, after adding sufficient cold water, stands the whole on an old or disused chair, log of wood, or anything else which will sufficiently heighten the same.

At the beginning of the twentieth century the large majority of Britain's cottages had no drainage: slops and other refuse were simply thrown out at the back, or in front, or into any convenient brook. Only in some of the larger villages was there a drain for surface water and kitchen slops.

Many families are pauperized [Green reported] on account of the amount of sickness produced by living under such unhealthy conditions, and many labourers become permanently disabled at a prematurely early age and have to be supported entirely by the rates for the remaining term of life, from the same cause.

Probably sheer undernourishment contributed in a similar degree.

Green's list of basic requirements for country cottages gives a good idea of existing conditions in 1900. There should be, he said, a closet or privy in the rear, a garden on which the household slops and excreta may be used and a pig housed and, in the kitchen, a grate substantial enough not to become quite unfit for use after a year or so. There should also be 'an arrangement on which the plates, cups etc., may be washed. This arrangement may be of metal, stone or brick cemented over. We prefer the stone . . . It should be connected from underneath one corner with, if possible, a drainage system; as, otherwise, if the waste water after washing up is run off into a pan or other receptacle, this, instead of being emptied with regularity, will certainly stand at times to ferment, and become a nuisance.' There should be 'a separate entrance to each bedroom, without it being necessary for the sleepers in different rooms to cross rooms other than their own'. Fireplaces should be so constructed that cottagers need not keep the door open from morning till night to get rid of smoke. Each room should have a window which will open.

General Sir Frederick Fitz Wygram is quoted on the subject of disposal for cottagers without drainage:

> A 36-gallon cask should be provided for the slops, about 6 feet from the back door. The cask should be raised 12 inches above the ground with a tap close to its bottom. This raising of the cask will enable a watering-pot to be placed under the tap. To enable the slops to be easily lifted into the cask, a step, one foot high . . . should be placed alongside the cask.

The slops were to be run off each day and sprinkled over parts of the garden by rotation. Considering how careless cottagers are reported to have been even with their sewage, it seems unlikely that many would have bothered with the cask system.

Insanitary matter lying about allowed a rapid spreading of certain diseases if infected people were present. A social worker reported of a cottage inhabited by a family of seven: 'I went into

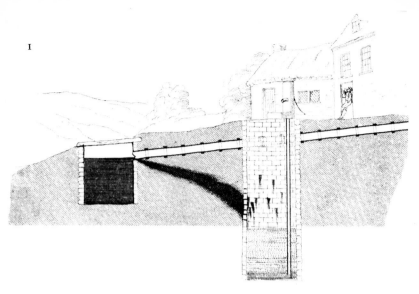

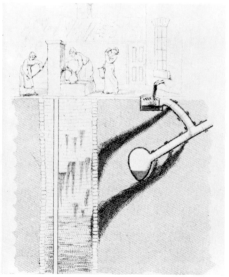

Illustrations entitled 'How people drink sewage', from T. Pridgin Teale's
Dangers to Health, *1878. 1. Full cesspool overflows into a nearby well.*
2. Drains leak into a well. Dr Pridgin Teale said that his drawings indicated
the condition of a probably large proportion of rural wells; he called for a
national organization to provide wholesome drinking water for villages.

59

this cottage one hot autumnal afternoon, when there was fever prowling near, to tell the poor man that his cottage was not fit for a dog or a pig to reside in, on account of the foul matters that were collected both in front and behind'. Three weeks later the social worker returned. 'The man was away, in the fields, at his work, but his wife and four children were sick in bed, in two little, close and badly ventilated chambers; the fifth child, a young girl, being alone left to nurse them.' He was there again a fortnight later. 'The girl who had been the nurse was then herself ill in bed with the fever, and she and her father were all that remained of the family of seven. Her mother and four brothers were all asleep beneath the sod of the churchyard . . . Thousands of people die in England in the same way every year'.

By the end of the nineteenth century most health authorities had come to the conclusion that, out in the country, earth closets offered the best method of dealing with sewage. Unfortunately cottagers tended to be careless over the drill for using them: a scoopful of dry earth was to be thrown into the pail after each use and the contents from time to time worked just below top soil in the garden. 'We have long advocated the use of the earth closet, or earth pail, in cottage dwellings', wrote Green. 'Still experience shows that it is very difficult indeed to get cottagers properly to use it, and the females seem to have a special repugnance to it.'

The disadvantage of the far more usual system, a privy perched above first one, then another hole in the ground, was contamination of the subsoil and in due course of the water in the well. Both such excavations were commonly sited just outside the back door. The architect William Bardwell wrote in *Healthy Homes* (1860):

> In the country it is almost incredible to see the universal contiguity of the pump and the cesspool or of the well and the cesspool. This is a mistake often fatal and always injurious to the health . . . Typhus, diarrhoea, and death are the frequent results of this thoughtless error. While surrounded on all sides by pure air, the sufferers are utterly at a loss to conjecture the cause of such oft-recurring sickness.

The first attempts in the 1870s to bring main drainage schemes to rural areas were carried out so badly that sometimes there was wholesale pollution of water supplies. When drains were laid in Brixworth districts of Northamptonshire – in seventeen of the thirty-six villages and hamlets – the results were disastrous; the chairman of the rural district council, Dr Cox, issued a public warning about the folly of water sewage schemes for ordinary villages. He had become convinced that the health of unsewered villages was better than that of the sewered ones. Drain pipes leaked, filtration beds became hopelessly clogged, and water-flushing of the sewers was either too much or too little. At Brixworth itself, sewered in 1877, the amount of spring water constantly getting into the drains was found to be copious enough to cover the whole area of the filtration bed two inches deep once in every twenty-four hours. It was stated that the effluent reaching an adjoining brook was at times 'singularly foul'.

All over rural England serious infections were inclined to spread like influenza, decimating village schools. The headmaster of a school in the small town of Arundel, Sussex, has left a day-by-day account of an epidemic of typhoid and dysentry in 1890. Again and again he refers to the sickly appearance of his pupils. 'A death', he says, 'occurs among them nearly every day.' The cause of the trouble turned out to be a clumsy opening of the ground to repair the main drain, leading to pollution of the water below the public pump. The pump was put under lock and key and in due course the epidemic died out.

But the origin of much of the nuisance from all these drainage schemes lay at the points of use. According to Dr Cox's report on Brixworth, in only one of the seventeen sewered villages were the closets technically water closets: they were just pan closets which could function reasonably well only if water was thrown down each day. Since the cottage housewife would not spare for this purpose water fetched from some distance, the pipes leading to the sewers remained unflushed, sometimes, from one year to another and frequently became completely choked. To sewer a village without providing for the flushing of each pan was, said Cox, a curse instead of a blessing. In the only village out of seventeen where the drains worked, the lavatories had cisterns.

Although knowing little about the way in which diseases are caught (organisms were not yet discovered), late nineteenth-century medical men confidently and correctly drew attention to running water supplies as likely carriers. The early mains water schemes, like the sewers, often caused outbreaks of serious disease. Having a tap to turn on could be a doubtful boon if the water behind it came direct and unfiltered from a small local river. Green writes of a fever-ridden village where mains water was obtained from the river at a point just above a waterfall two miles away. The water flowed directly into an iron pipe and was supplied to the village by gravity. The pressure in the pipes was inadequate in some parts of the village, not so much because of any shortage as because of the pipes getting blocked with river debris drawn into them. There was also much leakage.

An official who followed the course of the river for three and a half miles above the falls found 'abundant evidence of gross pollution' by sewage from another village which had a population of 447 and, moreover, contained a hotel. This village had no system of sewage and

> nearly the whole of the slop water and liquid refuse . . . and also the discharges from nearly all the water closets, are delivered directly or indirectly into the stream. In addition, privies are, where in use, in many instances built directly over small water courses falling to the river . . . The drainage from cowsheds, farmyards, manure heaps and stables also enters the river.

9

The Edwardian Poor

In some places in the early years of the twentieth century, farm labourers' wages were still at the eighteenth-century level of 11s a week. Christopher Holdenby in *Folk of the Furrow* gives a good idea of the life in rural cottages at that time, having lived in several as one of the family. Holdenby had chosen to work and lodge as a labourer by way of apprenticeship to an agricultural career. 'I became an excellent judge', he writes, 'of the flavour of potatoes. The great thing, if possible, is to find gravy from somewhere in which to crush the potatoes, and for this purpose my friends usually produced something they called meat.'

Holdenby estimated that there were thousands of cottages where they did not always see fresh meat once a week. In one cottage he lived in it was a great treat to open a tin of herrings on a Saturday night. Bad feeding, in his view, explained the sudden illnesses and short-delayed deaths of the labouring men:

> I have known men, subject to all weather conditions, go from morning till evening on a bread-and-butter pudding, and the evening meal was often a question of whether you wanted any . . . In a crisis my friends have nothing to fall back on. They look sunburnt and are often strong, but they are constantly suffering from chaps and chilblains – signs of more than mere exposure.

One of Holdenby's cupboard-like bedrooms held a bed, a washstand and a chair. He found it necessary to do most of his dressing in a crouching position on the bed. And this was a typical country cottage, he explains, not one of the 'real bad ones'. The latter kind were so numerous as to be unavoidable – though on big estates they were usually off the high road. In one village there was a row of four cottages where family seclusion was no longer possible. An occupant remarked: 'If you was to put a couple of pigs in the first parlour and their grub in the last, you could 'ave a rare good steeplechase right down the lot a-through the walls'.

Water was a common hazard. Holdenby once shared 'a modern estate cottage' and says of it:

> Not until the first dry summer did I discover that its water supply consisted in one small rainwater tank. Life is so simple in the cottage, and work so hard and often dirty, that we need plenty of water. We drink it, too ... My 'morning tub' – a distinctly necessary item after a day's manual labour – became a real difficulty, and I eventually discovered that I was drinking my own soapsuds regularly for supper.

According to a district nurse's account of cottage life in the Edwardian period – M. Loane's *An Englishman's Castle* (1909) – country people thought little of drinking tea made with rain water that had been standing three weeks in an open cask. She writes:

> I have known water used for cooking and drinking when it smelled so strongly that the same persons could not endure using it to wash the kitchen floor. Almost the first question one asks a cottage patient is, 'Where do you get water?', and a frequent reply is, 'We take it from the roadside in the winter, and in the summer they let us have it at the farm, but it's a dreadful long way to send, and the pump's out of order this year'.

An idea of standards of comfort in the country is offered by this exchange in Miss Loane's book: ' "Is your father comfortable in the almshouse?" I asked a very respectable, hard-working villager. "Well, he'd ought to be, miss. He has a boarded floor." ' Although no sort of luxury in the poorest town houses, boarded floors were still, in 1909, an amenity to be grateful for among country cottagers.

Miss Loane describes a cottage in a Norfolk village – a type of which there were plenty – inhabited by two elderly women, a widow and a spinster:

The ground floor consisted of a single, rather large room with an earthen floor as uneven as the worst of country lanes. There was a great cavern of a chimney, and in a small rusty grate a handful of sticks was smouldering. The walls had at one time been yellow-washed, but were so stained and broken that few traces of colour remained. There were no pictures and no ornaments, except two spotted dogs on the mantel-shelf. The furniture consisted of three wooden chairs without cushions and small bare table. The two women sat upright in front of the fireplace, with grimy, knotted hands resting on their knees; their short skirts were frayed and weather-stained, and muddy men's boots were on their feet. They both complained of rheumatism, of the difficulty of getting enough work, and of the approaching shadow of the dreaded workhouse.

It seems that they worked at weeding and stoning for a farmer at 8d a day.

Underpaid and exploited, the country labourers should have been either crushed or rebellious. They were neither. In *The Departed Village* (1968) R. E. Moreau quotes an octogenarian: 'People didn't know no different but to keep jigetting along; and whatever they were doing they were interested in. They were more *civilised* then.' But the exploitation and the need for decent cottages were coming to be widely discussed in the newspapers. Several energetic attempts were made by architects, builders and public-spirited members of the gentry to prove that a reasonable habitation could be built for £150, exclusive of the site. Such a cost enabled the cottage to be let at between 3s 6d and 4s, giving what was then a reasonable return on the money invested and allowing a small sum annually for repairs.

The building of Letchworth Garden City proved an excellent opportunity for architects to make practical experiments in cheap rural housing. In the Letchworth exhibition of 1905 there was a two-bedroom cottage, with parlour as well as living room, for which the building cost was reckoned at no more than a hundred guineas. Designed by F. W. Troup, it had a stud framework of home-grown fir and rested on a concrete raft.

In response to a challenge in the Press, Arnold Mitchell in 1913 published details of a couple of three-bedroom brick cottages, not

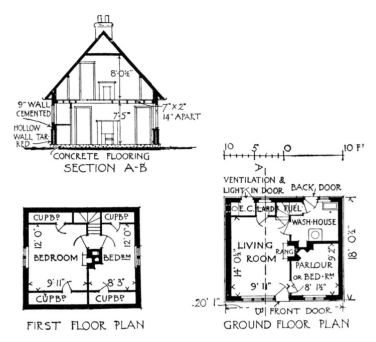

The Arnold Mitchell cottage built in 1913 for £110. From Lawrence Weaver's Book of Cottages, *1919.*

without faults, which he had had built at Merrow; again the cost was said to be a hundred guineas each. Each had nine-inch solid walls with a roof, pantile-covered, starting at first-floor level. This floor consisted of boards laid direct on the joists with no ceiling-work beneath; so anything spilled would tend to trickle straight through the boards and splatter the room below. The front door opened directly into the living room where the fireplace was set between this, the front door, and the doors to the washhouse and staircase; the cottager at his hearth would thus always be in a draught. The earth closet, reached through the outer door of the washhouse, was placed next to the larder.

A 1914 competition organized by *Country Life* for a pair of three-bedroom cottages at not more than £250 the pair produced interesting results, especially the design by W. Alex Harvey and H.

Graham Wicks which won first prize (Harvey designed most of the cottages at Bournville). Despite the extreme simplicity of the layout, it is clear from the plan that these cottages could be comfortable to live in. The third bedroom is downstairs, as is inevitable in the smallest type of cottage, but it does open from an entrance lobby inside the front door. The cost was kept within £250 by stipulating the use of reinforced concrete; in brick, the building was estimated to cost £281.

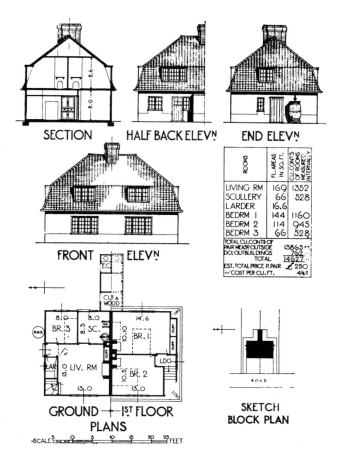

ROOMS	FL. AREAS IN SQ. FT.	CU. CONTS OF ROOMS MEASURED INTERNALLY
LIVING RM	169	1352
SCULLERY	66	528
LARDER	16.6	
BEDRM 1	144	1160
BEDRM 2	114	945
BEDRM 3	66	528
TOTAL CU. CONTS OF PAIR MEAS.º OUTSIDE		13865 FT
DO: OUTBUILDINGS		762
TOTAL		14627
EST. TOTAL PRICE P. PAIR		£250
·· COST PER CU. FT.		4½º

SECTION — HALF BACK ELEVⁿ — END ELEVⁿ

FRONT ELEVⁿ

GROUND — 1ST FLOOR PLANS

SKETCH BLOCK PLAN

A pair of cottages by W. Alex Harvey and H. Graham Wicks, estimated to cost £250. From Lawrence Weaver's Book of Cottages.

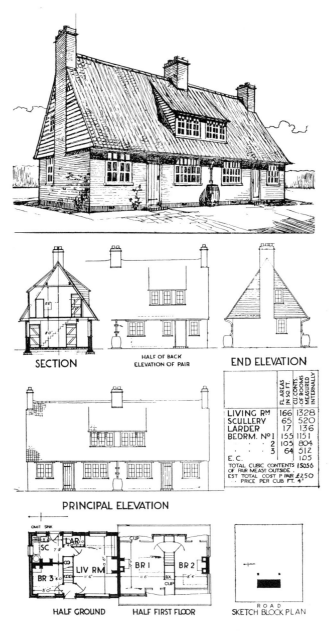

SECTION

HALF OF BACK
ELEVATION OF PAIR

END ELEVATION

PRINCIPAL ELEVATION

	FL. AREAS IN SQ.FT.	CU. CONTS. OF ROOMS MEASURED INTERNALLY
LIVING RM	166	1328
SCULLERY	65	520
LARDER	17	136
BEDRM. Nº1	155	1151
" " 2	105	804
" " 3	64	512
E.C.		105

TOTAL CUBIC CONTENTS 15056
OF PAIR MEASᵈ OUTSIDE .
EST TOTAL COST P PAIR £250
" PRICE PER CUB FT. 4ᵈ

OMIT SINK
LAR
SC
LIV RM
BR 3
CO
CUP
BR 1
BR 2
BX
CUP

HALF GROUND   HALF FIRST FLOOR

ROAD
SKETCH BLOCK PLAN

A pair of cottages by Courtney Crickmer, estimated to cost £250. From Lawrence Weaver's Book of Cottages.

68

It is hard to imagine, looking at the design, how the pair of cottages by Courtenay Crickmer could have been built for as little as £250 (in the 1960s such a building with three chimney stacks would cost £3,500); and indeed those who tried found they had to pay out well over £300. But perhaps it is more to the present purpose to draw attention to Crickmer's pleasantly clear-cut and functional rendering of a traditional design.

After the 1914-18 war the demand for rurally-placed cottages for labourers subsided: improved farm machinery meant that less men were needed to work on the land; and improved means of transport, especially the motor bicycle, meant that those who *were* needed could conveniently live in villages rather than on isolated sites among fields. The local councils became the main builders of these new village cottages, of which examples are never far to seek. Nearly always the ones that blend best with the villages they supplement are those which reflect some of the better, time-tested points of design from the past: a steeply pitched East Anglian roof, a Tudor gable, a Cotswold dormer. The better cottages are never faked to look old, nor are they the semi-reproductions of ancient models beloved by the Victorians – they are simply clean-lined and efficient modifications. The drawings in the second part of this book show a selection of the main types of cottage, built between 1450 and 1900, which, having survived, are to be seen today.

If most of this selection belongs to south-east England it is because this favoured part, susceptible to architectural influences from both London and the Low Countries, has always been a cradle of building styles for the rest of the country. In the eighteenth century it might take a new design a good fifty years to reach Northumberland, but the process became increasingly rapid. To compare a Kent village cottage built in 1890 with a Northumberland village cottage of the same date would be to see no difference, except that the one would probably be brick and the other stone. Regional variations are given less emphasis here than the broad development of shape and function.

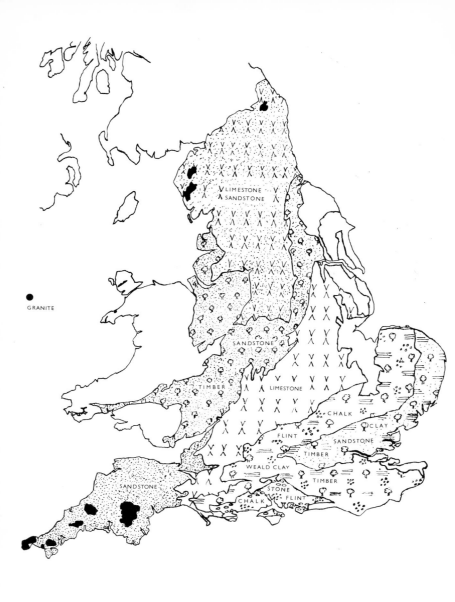

GRANITE

LIMESTONE
SANDSTONE

SANDSTONE

TIMBER

LIMESTONE

CHALK

CLAY

FLINT

SANDSTONE

TIMBER

WEALD CLAY

TIMBER

SANDSTONE

STONE

CHALK

FLINT

Distribution of the main building materials in England. Prepared by Douglas Relf.

Part Two

A Guide to
Types of Cottage

10

Fifteenth and
Sixteenth Centuries

Cruck c. 1450

The cruck cottage is one of the earliest types. In essence such a
building is all roof, the framework being pairs of tree trunks, or
crucks, which are stuck in the ground, tied at the top and linked
horizontally by a ridge pole. In examples that survive, upright
walls and a broader roof will have been added. The Nottingham-
shire cottage illustrated has brick nogging as a replacement for
some of the original in-filling of clay-daubed wattle, and adequate

73

glazed windows where once there were only tiny apertures with shutters. Originally there would have been no upper floor, and the smoke from a central hearth would have escaped as well as it could through a hole in the roof and through the windows (once known as 'wind-eyes').

The smallest house of this type had two pairs of crucks only. The space between them was known as a bay. This was usually between twelve and fifteen feet, a standard allowance based on the room needed for a team of four oxen. As buildings were taxed according to the number of bays, extensions tended to be little huts at the back rather than an extra bay.

Because of its simplicity, a form of cruck construction, seen best today in old barns, was still being used as late as the eighteenth century, especially by squatters who had to make themselves shelters in a hurry; but after about 1500 crucks were superceded for all serious building by the box frame, sometimes called 'post and truss' or 'post and panel'. Examples of pre-1600 date would not have sheltered poor peasants; their cottages have not survived because they were too flimsily built, having never been intended – so it can be deduced from manorial court rolls – to last more than about one generation. Knowledge of these tiny cottages is derived from archaeological excavations.

Box Frame with Jetty c. 1530

Thousands of box-framed timber houses and cottages are still to be seen. Their raftered roofs are supported on a framework of vertical posts, known as studs, and of horizontal beams. Beneath there are brief footing walls of rubble or brick rising about twelve inches from the ground. In the common term 'half-timbered', the 'half' refers only to the material used to fill in 'the framework'.

Timber-framed buildings with studs that are set close together – as in this Suffolk example – are generally found to belong to the period of roughly 1550-1660, when oak was still plentiful and cheap. However a *starting* date of 1450 might not be unreasonable. Until recently it was accepted that the carpenter-made buildings of the South East, put up in the middle of the sixteenth century, founded a style which spread throughout the country. But J. T. Smith, writing in the *Archaeological Journal* in 1966, contends that this was not so; that there were, all along, two schools which developed separately – the south-eastern and the western.

The most noticeable feature of Tudor timber buildings is the projection on one or more sides of the upper storey. This was built separately and might project as much as four feet. The reason for this construction, known as the jetty, was principally to give stability to floors whose joists were in those days laid flat instead of on their edges. It was found that the weight of an upper wall set down on the protruding ends of these joists counteracted satisfactorily the weight of people and furniture inside the building. It is probable that a jettied upper storey was also thought useful in helping to protect the lower one from the effects of rain water. The buildings had no gutters or down pipes.

Another important reason for jettying is that if it was necessary to go higher than one storey, it was not ordinarily possible to get enough long timbers to run right through. Arranging short vertical timbers in jetties produced a stronger article than keeping them on one vertical plane.

Box Frame with Concealed Jetty c. 1550

An example of a Tudor jettied building (Somerset) now serving as cottages. It has had its recessed lower wall filled out flush with brickwork – probably because the ends of the joists were decayed and beginning to sag. Had the building been given a coating of plaster, it would be difficult to tell from the outside that a jettied construction existed. Indoors, though, one would notice that the front wall was curiously thick. These cottages appear to have seventeenth-century windows with leadwork retaining small pieces of glass – the only kind easily available. The first windows would have been of open latticework in wood supplemented by shutters for keeping out rain and draughts. Shutters continued in use to deter intruders long after windows began to be glazed late in the sixteenth century. Sometimes they are still so employed today.

Balloon Frame c. 1590

The jetty and the making of each storey separately was abandoned early in the seventeenth century.[1] Henceforth timber builders favoured box- or balloon-frame constructions, which had long existed alongside jettied constructions; in this the upright members rose direct from a sleeper resting on a footings wall to the ends of the roof rafters. The whippiness of the floor timbers, still laid flat, was now counteracted by heavy cross beams.

The popularity of this new method of framing was partly stimulated by an alleged timber shortage. Numerous tall studs placed close together were unnecessary when more horizontal beams were used. The interstices of the framework became roughly square (and suitable for forming windows): they were filled, as before, with panels of hurdle sprung into place in grooves and then daubed on both sides.

The idea of a timber shortage seems curious in the light of a contemporary estimate that England had an acreage of woodland

[1] This mode of building seems to have persisted longest in East Anglia. It was used for much of the rebuilding of Wymondham, Norfolk, after a fire in 1610.

of about three million in the last quarter of the sixteenth century – enough to completely cover four counties. In Sussex oak grew like a weed. However, Queen Elizabeth's government had become worried by heavy felling of oak – one of its uses was as a fuel in iron making – and by the thought that there might not be enough to build the ships to repel a threatened invasion by Spain. Economy in domestic building was the result of a government order.

Balloon Frame with Chimney Stack c. 1600

The effect of square panels, especially when the wood was blackened as it was in the Midlands, the West and the North, may be less attractive than closely studded work, but there is no doubt that this type of framework, born of shortage, was more scientifically designed. The Herefordshire cottage shown is

79

severely black and white, and demonstrates the rather crude way in which masonry chimney stacks were attached to the outside of a gable end as though an afterthought. Sometimes, of course, the chimney *was* an afterthought, but this cottage is not the simple dwelling with central hearth which would have acquired its first real chimney as a later improvement. The oven, shown protruding from the base of the stack and having its own lean-to roof, probably dates from as late as 1800: not many cottages could afford to bake bread till then. The door of the oven would be to one side of a capacious fireplace.

Plastered Box Frame c. 1550

The slightly cocked-up ends of the roof ridge of this Hertfordshire box frame cottage denote eastern counties thatch. An inspection of the oak framework behind a complete cladding of laths and plaster reveals uprights set within a few inches of each other, indicating that the cottage was built well before the need to economize on oak at the end of the sixteenth century. The central chimney stack rises from a single very large hearth. There are two rooms on the left of this stack and one on its right, the three conforming with a usual pattern: best parlour, eating parlour or kitchen, store (nearest the artist). Two bedrooms formed in the roof space are reached by a boxed-in staircase against a partition wall. The windows are comparatively modern.

Tudor House Converted c. 1550

A typical timber-framed and jettied Tudor house in a village street (Hertfordshire) which has long done duty as a row of cottages. The old village farmhouses often became redundant as a result of eighteenth-century enclosures and the merging of farms, and were divided into the maximum number of dwellings for labourers. Such buildings may be seen lining the streets of numerous villages; there are also many examples in isolated positions.

The type of house drawn, mediaeval in origin, became a standard pattern. The three sections, hall part in the middle flanked by double-storeyed wings set at right angles, made them fairly easy to convert; though the landlord would be lucky if he did not have to provide two extra chimney stacks.

When the hall part is of early date it will show signs of having had originally no upper floor; there might have been a mere hole between the rafters for letting out smoke from a fire in the middle of the floor. The jettying-out of the cross wings would have been, as explained earlier, to increase the stability of the upper floor, a common practice in the building of timber-framed houses before the seventeenth century. The windows are of sash type and larger than the Tudor casements that preceded them.

II

Seventeenth Century

Cornish Longhouse c. 1650

The longhouse is a type belonging to the north and west; it provides living accommodation and an animals' shelter under a single extended roof line. Longhouses are not found in the South-East. In the more rugged parts of the British Isles, where rocks are thick on the moorlands and in the beds of rivers, cottages like this have an organic, local quality that makes them hard to date. The Cornish type drawn, with its massive walls (and brief interior), could be as early as the fifteenth century or as late as the eighteenth. So rude a shelter for all the events of family life at least boasted a sound fireplace; though in a treeless district there was the constant problem of what to burn in it. Dried dung from animals was often used.

For hundreds of years Cornish cottages were built of unhewn pieces of granite, large and small. No mortar was used, though the boulders were either bedded in mud or had mud pushed between them later to keep out rain and wind. Examples with roofs of flat stones or of thatch are to be seen in the Isle of Man, North Wales, the Scottish highlands and on Dartmoor.

Building walls without mortar (or even mud) is an ancient art which is still usefully practiced: thousands of miles of such walls run across the countryside in the west and the north-west. The builders of them are known as dry dykers. Colonel Rainsford Hannay writes in *Dry Stone Walling* (1957) of a middle-aged dry dyker who asked his priest what the D.D. after his name meant. 'Doctor of Divinity', he was told. A few days later the man had to sign a document in the presence of the priest and added the letters D.D. to his signature. 'Dry dyker' he explained. 'But that's not a profession', said the priest. 'You're right, Minister. It's an art'. One of the arts is the handling of a two-inch board in such a way that with its leverage two men can handle boulders as large as cabin trunks.

Cotswold Limestone c. 1625

A Cotswold cottage built with a concern for architectural detail that would rarely be bestowed in other regions on so small a house. But the charms of the Cotswold masonry need, as they say, little introduction. The distinctive style, based on a tradition handed on by generations of village craftsmen, was established at the beginning of the seventeenth century; it was made possible by excellent supplies of good local limestone and money earned by the wool trade.

The predominant structural feature of this part of England is the Cotswold dormer, formed by carrying the main wall up to form a gable. This usually has a roof ridge nearly as high as that of the building itself. Often there are several such gables in a row. The other characteristic features are chimney stacks with bold cornices (good sites for house martin nests), and long mullioned windows. Even quite humble cottages had carefully chiselled drip mouldings above the windows. Iron casements, some of them hinged, were fitted between the mullions when, after about 1575, glazing became common in all but the smallest cottages.

Boarded Box Frame c. 1650

There is no external treatment which can make it harder to identify an old cottage than weather-boarding.

These cottages shown in the heart of a Kent village, with Georgian pediments over their doors, and generally eighteenth-century in shape, give little hint on the outside that they date from about the middle of the seventeenth century, and that beneath the boarding there is a framework of oak.

The terms weather-boarding and clapboarding both refer to the method of fixing planks horizontally in such a way that they overlap one another. This form of cladding effectively gave extra warmth and protection from the elements. It has long been characteristic of cottages in the three south-eastern counties, and especially Kent.

Farmhouse Type c. 1650

By the seventeenth century the bigger cottages were being built
in the same general shape as the farmhouses; they would be of a
single span with a chimney stack in the middle. But this stack was
rarely quite central. Country people were not yet symmetry-
conscious, and they found it convenient to have their ground
floor rooms of unequal size. Whatever happened, the kitchen had
always to be bigger than the parlour. Having the stack *inside* the
building, instead of attached to an outside wall, was considered a
fine new invention which tended to conserve warmth indoors. It
would be built first of all and serve, if the cottage was otherwise of
timber, to steady the whole structure; it also acted as a support for
the staircase.

Western Thatched c. 1650

Another seventeenth-century farmhouse type, with a hipped roof, and a prominent chimney stack which divides the lower floor into two unequal portions. An extra stack has been added – at a date suggested by the Victorian chimney pot. The groundfloor casement windows are of a usual eighteenth-century kind. It is likely that originally all windows had small leaded panes like those of the upper window nestling in its gable of thatch. As a means of lighting attic rooms, pleasant looking gablets like these were much easier to construct than dormer windows.

Where cottage walls, especially the front wall, are unexpectedly thick – say two feet – it may well turn out that a brick facing has been built over a timber framework.

Eastern Thatched c. 1690

A two-roomed Suffolk cottage, with the kitchen-living room on the left and the sleeping chamber on the right; brick-built it would have been very superior in its day.

Reed thatch of the type shown ornamented with scallops and uncomplicated by window openings, is rare outside East Anglia. Suffolk in particular is still a region where the inherited skill of the thatcher shows itself in taut, crisp-lined work that is different from the style of the west. According to a Rural Community Council survey of 1960, this county has more thatch than any other. Thatch is of course little use in trying to date a building, since even reeds, the best variety, have to be renewed, or at least supplemented, about every forty years, while wheat straw has only half the life. Originally reed thatching was restricted to the valleys of the main rivers, the Fens and the Broads of East Anglia. In central Norfolk and Suffolk one still finds thatch of wheat straw.

Economy Timber c. 1650

Cottages like this demonstrate the lowered carpentry standards of the seventeenth century. The carpenter-builders used roughly shaped and irregular lengths of oak, put in diagonal braces here and there and generally gave up any attempt at a sensible pattern. The spaces were now sometimes filled in with brickbats, whose weight encouraged the familiar bulging of timber-framed walls. Nevertheless, thousands of these buildings have survived three centuries – and with the aid of steel tie rods some may last several more. Very often their builders had the grace to cover them over with plaster, thereby concealing the carpentry and keeping out some of the draughts. In East Anglia much of the post-mediaeval framing was designed from the start to be plastered.

Somerset Stone c. 1680

In stone-building areas the axial chimney stack never became usual. The cottage shown is a type common in Somerset, at the southern end of the limestone belt which runs from the Wash down to Dorset. The front door is formed in the same gable end as the chimney stack. The meagre height of this door, making it impossible for most adults to enter without stooping, is a reminder of how much people's average height has increased.

On entering the main room, one would find a thin partition dividing off a smaller, unheated room beyond, originally a buttery, parlour or sleeping-place – or all three. Above are two inter-communicating bedrooms. The builders of stone dwellings took no chances with windows and put in mullions robust enough to carry heavy loads. The purpose of the decorative lip moulding above windows was to throw off rain water.

Rubble Stone c. 1625

A humbler version of the preceding cottage, and one which may well have been put together by its first inhabitant. One notes the haphazard positions and sizes of the windows. But to most seventeenth-century labourers this cottage would have seemed very superior accommodation. It is possible that no use was made of the roof space when the cottage was first built. When sleeping lofts were made later, the usual way of reaching them was by ladder. The round projection at the nearer gable end, thatched like the roof, is an oven built within the hearth – and almost certainly an early eighteenth-century addition.

Cob c. 1650

At one time cottages built of mud existed all over England, but in the south-west, and especially in Devon, this method of building was widespread. Even today it is possible in Devon to find whole villages made of mud, which is referred to there as 'cob'. All cob needs, according to an ancient and much quoted adage, is a good hat and a good pair of shoes – that is to say, a thatched roof generous enough to throw the rain clear and a foundation of stone. In fact cob cottages plastered over, or simply given a hard skin with repeated coats of whitewash, have lasted for centuries. Door and window frames need to be of stout construction, of course, and vulnerable angles are the better for being rounded.

Chalk was valued as an ingredient for mud walling. In a letter to *The Times* in 1927, Thomas Hardy described the procedure as he remembered it:

What was called mud-wall was really a composition of chalk, clay and straw – essentially unbaked brick. This was mixed up into a sort of dough-pudding close to where the cottage was to be built. The mixing was performed by treading and shovelling – women sometimes being called in to tread – and the straw was added to bind the mass together. . . . It was then thrown by pitchforks on to the wall, where it was trodden down to a thickness of about two feet, till a rise of about three feet had been reached. This was left to settle for a day or two . . .

Single-storey dwellings, with walls about six feet high, could thus be thrown up quite quickly (though paring down with a shovel and finishing touches would be done at leisure), but for superior two-storey cottages as much as a year might be allowed for the proper drying of each course. The type of external chimney-stack of the cottage drawn, and the small-paned casement windows (not all of which open), were common in the west till well into the eighteenth century.

Converted Farmhouse c. 1650

In numerous old villages it will be found that most of the central cottages are carved out of village-street farmhouses dating from pre-enclosure days. Beneath the chimney stack of this rather battered-looking, plastered building (Cambridgeshire) there was once a commodious farm kitchen where living-in farmhands had their meals with the farmer. For a long time now it has accommodated cottages and a shop. The typically Regency shop window, dating from about 1810, is probably the most recent external alteration.

These single-span houses, like the Tudor farmhouse already discussed, were ideal for conversion. Some were converted to ale-houses. New doorways presented no problem, and steep stairs were easily enough inserted for reaching the upper floor.

Subdivided Cottage c. 1650

Cottages are often older than they seem from the outside. Tiles may hang where once there was thatch and modern boards may completely cover ancient walls. Behind the blackened weatherboarding of this Hertfordshire cottage there is a seventeenth-century oak frame. Originally it would have been a dwelling up to the standard of a small farmer's house with a single front door. It was probably converted for the use of two families in the first half of the nineteenth century. Although each family had its own front door, they were obliged to use the same steep, semi-circular stair case situated at the far side of the large central stack. Upstairs there are two intercommunicating bedrooms.

Georgian-fronted Vernacular

The towns and villages of the south-east are abundantly stocked with buildings that appear to belong to the eighteenth century but are really older. The dislike of the Georgians for half-timber work and their enthusiasm for the regular, classical look led to ceaseless alteration. Often cottages as well as houses were redressed to look modern. And with the aid of weather boarding, various kinds of tile, or sometimes whole facades of solid brick, it was possible to hide away the out-of-date timber of the past.

The Kent village cottage shown is a good example of a seventeenth-century building (with parts that may be considerably older) which has had the Georgian treatment. The builder was unable to achieve full Georgian regularity – the sash windows are neither equal in size nor at the regulation distances from each other – but at least he had created a general effect in tune with the modern taste of his time. Today there is sense of surprise on walking into an apparently Georgian cottage to find a huddle of ancient rooms and a great ingle-nooked fireplace.

12

Eighteenth Century

Welsh Traditional c. 1700

The lowest common denominator among detached cottages (with just two rooms and a hearth), this type is to be seen with various roof coverings all over Europe; it remains a not uncommon dwelling even in the English Home Counties; it is very common in France. In the highlands of Scotland, and of course Ireland, the building of simple one-storey cottages remained normal long after the end of the eighteenth century. Very often the first occupier did the building with his own hands, perhaps with help provided by the tenant farmer for whom he worked. In country parts he had no plumbing or drainage arrangements to bother about, none being needed, though he would hope to find a supply of water within, say, a quarter of a mile. Otherwise a shallow rain-water well often sufficed.

Essex Verge c. 1780

Another basic cottage with a shape that anyone building himself something to live in might almost instinctively put together. There are still plenty of huts like this on scraps of ground, formerly waste, beside main roads. Beneath the weather-boarding and the patent Roman tiles (a flatter version of the pantile) this one has an ancient yet tolerably sound oak frame. Since it was erected some 200 years ago, the level of the road has risen. A screen provides two rooms leading out of one another; very often there was no such subdivision.

It was more usual for these verge cottages to have the door to the right-hand side of the wall facing the road. Immediately inside, to the right, would be a little pantry and beyond it stairs up to a cramped loft.

Cornish Vernacular c. 1700

Many cottages of the less sophisticated regions of England undoubtedly came into existence through communal activity. In Cornwall fishermen and their neighbours helped one another to put together rustic dwellings of rubble stone and slate of the kind drawn. The extreme hardness of the local shales and bits of granite helped to give their handiwork a distinctive character. These cottages are hard to date, for traditional local methods were followed for century after century.

It was usual west-country practice to place the main chimney stack on a side wall near the front door. The fireplace within would consist of two large stone slabs, with another slab for a lintel, standing on a raised hearth. Peat and furze were the normal fuel.

Estate Foreman's Popular c. 1780

The cottage specifically built for foremen and other favoured estate workers by a professional builder was a new type of house dating from the middle of the eighteenth century. Country squires, always particular about stabling for their horses, were beginning to show some concern for the housing of their human workers. The Surrey cottage drawn is typical of the plain kind of improved cottage; the sweeping down of the main roof at the back forms an outshut for use as a scullery; the four front rooms are poky, square and low-ceilinged. Because cottages of this sort have survived, it is often forgotten that only a fraction of eighteenth–century land workers were so well housed.

The tax on glass was not allowed to disturb an orderly array of front windows on the better cottages; the economical absence of windows on the gable walls was partly the result of chimneys rising up the middle. The smooth line of gable ends was made possible by the Georgian practice of letting these chimney stacks project inside instead of on the outside of exterior walls. This arrangement was by no means unknown, however, in the seventeenth century.

Brick and Stud c. 1790

A type localized in the south-east, this brick and stud cottage has
the same basic design as the previous cottage, and with the same
kind of neat hood over the front door; but except that the roof has
been hipped and tiles hung on the upper storey. Tiles usually
cover a timber framework, and those here may have been applied
subsequently as a weather-proofing sheath. Since this is a late
Georgian cottage, the framework timber is probably softwood. In
the days when bricks were both taxed and expensive to transport it
could be a worthwhile saving to halt the brickwork half way up and
carry on with wood.

Norfolk Farm Worker's c. 1780

An East Anglian cottage of brick and flint which conforms closely to Georgian ideas about regularity. On entering Norfolk, Suffolk and parts of Cambridge and Huntingdonshire one notices plenty of flint, though the greater number of East Anglian cottages are still the framed type, plastered over and thatched. Steeply pitched roofs are plentiful: thatch and pantiles, the customary roof coverings, both need a steep slope to throw off the rain quickly.

Pantiles, which have been sent over from the Low Countries since the end of the seventeenth century, became the universal kind of tile in East Anglia. (Where a pantiled roof has high gables – above the tiles as here – its original covering was probably thatch.) Pantiles interlock transversely, the bent-over edge of one pantile hooking over the bent-up edge of its neighbour. Although much stouter than plain tiles, pantiles make a lighter roof through being arranged with less overlapping. They have often been used to replace thatch. It is difficult to form a satisfactory verge with pantiles: hence the parapeted gable end.

The steepness of East Anglian roofs made it impossible to extend the slope at the back to take in an extension of usable height; outshuts are therefore separately roofed and often on a gable wall. Laying wedges of brickwork at right angles to the line of the gable parapet is known as tumbling; it is of Dutch origin and is especially common in Norfolk.

Eastern Semi-Detached c. 1790

The semi-detached arrangement was largely a late eighteenth-century innovation which came out of efforts by a minority of landlords to provide improved housing for their farm workers.[1] It was obviously economical to build like this, and tenants said they liked the companionship of another family living on the other side of the central chimney stack. This cottage in Lincolnshire is a less usual type; it boasts a separate stack for each cottage. It

[1] Mr. A. P. Baggs states that he has 'looked at a pair of houses (dated 1675 on the structure) which appear to have been semis from the start. I have also seen documentary evidence of semis in Cambridgeshire dating from the late seventeenth century'.

differs from the Norfolk Cottage in having no dormer windows and an outshut washhouse at one end instead of the back.

The practice of building cottages in pairs, which became very common in Victorian times, seems to have spread from the eastern counties. For the glory of the landowner who ordered them, they were sometimes arranged prominently along a lane.

Labourers' Terrace c. 1730

The building of labourers' cottages in rows, or terraces, is a comparatively modern idea. This early eighteenth-century row in Cambridgeshire, with two main rooms in each dwelling, is believed to be one of the first of its type. The gable end shows the method of arranging bricks known as tumbling; it is rarely seen outside the eastern counties. As with most rural cottages having more than one floor, the upper rooms are contained in the roof space. The almost casual sweeping of the thatch round the windows of these produces an example of the less fussy type of gablet.

Farmhouse Type c. 1790

One of the more commodious of the early Georgian cottage types, it is common in the south-east. The original occupant is more likely to have been a small farmer than a labourer. Full oak frameworks were now obsolete for all but the meaner cottages. In stoneless rural areas, bricks would be made on the spot wherever the soil held enough clay. The pit created by digging for it often became a pond.

Cottage builders were beginning to follow the Renaissance shapes which were the rage in house design, and strove after regularity in elevation and plan. But though sash windows were now the only permitted kind for houses, cottages usually had simple casements with solid wood frames. In the south, roofs were commonly hipped, as shown.

Fireplaces were now being put at either end of most detached cottages, but the builder of this one (no architect is likely to have come near it) clings to the central chimney stack of the seventeenth century. Unlike his predecessors, however, he has put it in the exact centre to avoid upsetting his symmetrical elevation. As a result the kitchen, instead of being usefully larger than the parlour, is the same size. The middle window was either filled in to avoid window tax or – and this is just as likely at the close of the eighteenth century – designed to be a blocked window to give relief to what would otherwise be a large expanse of brickwork.

The absence of any visible chimney pot was usual in the early eighteenth century. When the largely unnecessary pot came into general use after about 1750, the better builders sank it so that only about two inches projected. This was enough to give the wind a chance to blow across the edges and thereby increase draughts up the flue.

Transitional Georgian c. 1775

This substantial cottage in Yorkshire is in fact only a two–bedroom type. The sash windows indicate a conscious attempt at elegance. Humbler cottages in Yorkshire and many other parts had frames that slid from side to side. These are generally called Yorkshire sliding sashes, though they are very common in Cambridgeshire and other counties as well.

The builder has adopted the fashion of the south in forming a chimney stack in each gable end; the arrangement left room for a convenient staircase in the middle of the cottage and for a through passage from the front door to the back. He has not, however, reduced the size of the kitchen to that of the parlour, and he has had in consequence to pay the price of having a facade which is less than symmetrical.

Northern Granite c. 1760

The Georgian fashions of the south took some fifty years to reach the extreme north of England, but the builder of the squat, double-fronted stone cottage, with its chimney at each end, has made some attempt at a balanced front. All the same, by keeping the front door slightly to one side – as in the preceding example – he has allowed for the kitchen to be the largest room.

The hard granites, limestones and slates of Westmorland and much of the northern region are friable and difficult to work, and largely account for the characteristic ruggedness of the housing. The heavy roofing stones were carried on stout rafters set at a shallow pitch to reduce the danger of slipping. Door and window openings were commonly made from single blocks of dark gritstone. Chimney pots were fashioned with slips of stone.

Mansard-roofed Semi c. 1790

To give servants more headroom in their attic bedrooms, the mansard type of roof shown above, pantile-covered, became a not unusual feature among new Georgian houses. It was taken up by a number of cottage-builders in the last quarter of the century. The lower slope was often too steep for pantiles, which are held by nibs instead of pegs or nails, and a common arrangement was to have plain tiles below and pantiles on the shallow top pitch. This double-pitch roof is characteristically French, though it is now believed that there was no justification for naming it after the seventeenth-century French architect F. Mansard. Construction and maintenance of mansards gave more trouble than single-pitch roofs, and they were rarely put on Victorian cottages. The example is in Lincolnshire.

Weaver's c. 1785

According to which way you look at it, this weaver's cottage has either twelve windows to its upper storey or one very large one divided by eleven stone mullions. The point would have been important to the eighteenth-century owner, since window tax – first imposed in 1696 and not abolished until 1851 – was levied according to the number of openings on any dwelling worth over £5 a year.

A lengthy array of window panes to light the room which housed the loom is an arresting feature of the thorough-going weaver's cottage. The stone-built example shown is near Huddersfield, Yorkshire. Geoffrey N. Wright, who supplied the photograph from which the drawing was made, writes that conversions and restorations are changing many of these old cottages though this one still retains its essential character. Under the domestic system of industry, weaving and spinning went on in a big way in the homes of the poor. Needless to say the majority of these homes lacked the convenience of large windows.

Gothic Revival Lodge c. 1760

Horace Walpole's treatment of Strawberry Hill, his house at Twickenham, helped to win favour for a revival of the Gothic style (it was revived again in the nineteenth century); basically the system is structural, with arches and component parts made conspicuously ornamental. Fashionable landlords often ordered the Gothic style for those cottages on their estates which would be sure to catch the traveller's eye. To this day they provoke second glances.

The rough-cast Wiltshire cottage drawn boasts a wealth of Gothic pointed arches along with vaguely Eastern battlements, and it has, on the upper floor, quatrefoil windows in iron tracery similar to specimens at Strawberry Hill. The designs for Gothic revival lodges and other small buildings were taken from pattern books which, after about 1770, even exhibited Gothic versions of buildings in the East. Mediaeval novels of the period, like Walpole's *Castle of Otranto*, greatly encouraged a general desire for styles of the past and of far-away places. Even the classical architect Robert Adam produced Gothic designs when asked.

Model Cottages c. 1775

Milton Abbas, Dorset, was one of the eighteenth-century model villages where, in a period of widespread dereliction, the high standard of labourers' housing was a wonder to all. This village was laid out to rehouse families evicted through the demolition of the old village of Milton Abbas – which the squire had decided was unattractively near his house. The square-thatched cottages, formal in design yet owing something to the Picturesque cult, line a long broad road that climbs gently through wooded country. They have been kept as they were, apart from minor alterations. Their record as living accommodation is a full one. In 1841, for example, each cottage was being lived in by four families, an average of thirty-six people per dwelling.

13

Nineteenth Century

Lock-Keeper's Picturesque c. 1810

The Regency style (roughly 1800-1835) was a frivolous, dainty and often attractive version of the Georgian style. Designers made play with simulated columns and recessed areas of brickwork; they liked rounded walls, bow windows, balconies and verandahs with slender cast-iron pillars. Bricks were either concealed beneath stucco or washed over with a pale colour. Roofs were nearly flat and had enormous eaves.

Regency generally brings to mind the better kind of small villa architecture and certain terraces of houses in London, Cheltenham and Brighton. But here and there a workman's cottage, as shown, would be carefully designed to fit in with the fashion. Such a cottage can also be thought of as a variant of the Picturesque.

Gothic Revival c. 1810

This self-conscious lodge containing two minute rooms clearly belongs to the early nineteenth-century: it mixes the classical manner in its shallow slated roof with the Gothic in the shape of the door and of the ogee-arched windows. Whether the walls were of soft-wood studs, bricks or clay lumps, the usual wish at this period was that they should be stuccoed. Little structures like this were sometimes put up as garden houses.

Workman's Regency c. 1825

A standard cottage shape of the early nineteenth century, strictly two rooms up and two down, which is to be seen in both town and country as far apart as Kent and Wales. The Regency taste shows itself in the shape of the sharply projecting roof and in the stuccoed brickwork marked out to resemble stone. The blocked-up window is a familiar reminder of the tax on windows. Cobbett derided the fashion for little white boxes which seemed to him effete and artificial as well as insubstantial. Certainly stucco often concealed some very poorly-done brickwork of the nine-inch-solid variety.

The introduction of Welsh slates at the end of the eighteenth century helped classically-minded builders to pitch their roofs as low as possible: the closely fitting slates made it possible to achieve a pitch as low as 25 degrees, as in the illustration. Roofs of this sort are a most noticeable feature of early nineteenth-century buildings.

The appeal of stucco as a facing material spread all over Britain in the period 1810-1850. This external rendering generally consisted of Parker's Roman cement, which was harder and less coarse than previous plasters. It was superceded in the mid-nineteenth century by Portland cement, which was easier to work though starker in appearance. However, by this time public opinion was beginning to turn against any sort of facing for brick-work on the ground that it was dishonest. Trade in neater-looking bricks, machine-made, flourished.

Tollkeeper's Octagonal c. 1805

Octagonal cottages appeared in several of the early nineteenth-century pattern books directed to estate owners and the rich in general. Architects thought the shape neat and romantic; they do not appear to have thought much about the difficulties it imposed on arranging furniture. But in the Yorkshire example here, one sees an octagonal cottage serving a useful purpose: its generous windows command just the views needed by the man who opened the turnpike gates and took the money for passage. In style the cottage is an example of the transitional phase between the Georgian and the Victorian.

Gatekeeper's Old English c. 1830

The cult of the Picturesque (which by 1830 was merging into that of the Romantic) was responsible for numerous whimsical and often inconvenient gatekeepers' cottages, though not as many as one might suppose from the array of contemporary design published. Most architects considered thatch essential for suggesting the rustic and the mediaeval. For the same reason leaded lights in lattice form was in favour for windows; often these were not made to open. When kept in order, these smaller manifestations of mediaeval revivalism retain a certain period charm.

Railwayman's Romantic c. 1850

The railway companies took some pains in their early days with the design of the stations and other buildings that skirted their tracks. The Romantic manner, successor to the Picturesque, cropped up in all the pattern books; and this seemed to the railway builders exactly what was wanted to mark the adventure of a method of travel faster than had ever been known. Thus the humblest track-side cottage was given the 'Old English' look and as many emotive touches as cheapness would allow.

The crossing keeper's cottage shown, with its carved barge boards under the eaves of the gable and cement dressings to the windows and angles, is in Kent, but the type can be seen all over the British Isles. The 'Old English' style was, indeed, national, departing in both planning and appearance from the traditional and locally identified types. Archaeologically the style had barely any foundation in fact, but was a work of the architects' imagination which seems to have been influenced by European models as much as English. Cottages like the one shown may be readily seen in France fulfilling the same function. The stucco now shunned in England as dishonest might have helped the nine-inch solid walls to keep out the rain: instead they have at some time been given a coating of tar.

Softwood Regency c. 1805

The covering of old oak-framed buildings with softwood planks
from Scandinavia led to the economical use of softwood for the
whole frames of new cottages. At the end of the eighteenth century,
and during the Regency, numerous cottages of this sort appeared

in the south and east, especially in fishing villages. They were weatherboarded more often than tiled. The construction was not only cheap; it beat the brick tax which was introduced in 1784 and not repealed until 1850.

The cottage drawn (Kent) is entirely wooden except for a brick base, chimney stacks and the lean-to shed. The latter was probably an afterthought. For the sake of economy the rear chimney (also an afterthought) is formed of bricks laid on their sides. The view from behind shows a Georgian method of roof construction, copied from house-building, which allowed a cottage to be fatter than was possible with the normal single-span roof – that is, to have a double depth of rooms. But valleys often become clogged with leaves and water, and eventually cottages of two rooms deep were covered with a single tall roof of wide span. The sash windows on the rear wall, squat to suit the low height of the rooms, are later additions. The view of the front of the cottage demonstrates one drawback to casement windows – the awkward appearance they present when fully open.

Softwood Semi c. 1835

Another deal-framed building with external weather-boarding (Surrey). Cheaply-built pairs like this, each having two rooms on the ground floor, one behind the other, and each served by the one central chimney stack, were typical of run-of-the-mill housing for farm-workers in the south. The full two storeys, instead of one storey and attics, shows that they were not quite rock bottom types. By the beginning of Queen Victoria's reign sash windows had become almost standard fittings for cottages.

The semi-detached design is one of the few inventions that spread from cottages to houses instead of the other way round. During the Victorian period cottages and houses in pairs, commonly described as villas, went up all over the British Isles.

Scottish Popular c. 1845

Throughout the nineteenth century the building of single storey cottages remained widespread; but until the bungalow came into fashion (with a Hindu name to show it was different) no one in England supposed that the single-storey dwelling was anything other than inferior to the kind with an upper floor, even if this was just an attic with a window. In Scotland the point of view was different: two-storeyed cottages were scarcely ever built till late in the century, and even in the towns Scottish custom decreed that people lived in flats where the English would live in tall terrace houses with two rooms to each floor.

The Scottish cottage illustrated dates from the mid-nineteenth century, yet is built to a centuries-old pattern (employed, more or less, for the turf-walled huts) which had changed as little as the way of life of the rural workers. The interior would consist – and in places it still does today – of a single room fitted with built-in box beds. A big improvement for some of the village cottages in the later nineteenth century was a piped water supply. There would be a pump or standpipe on the curb to serve several households.

New-style Scottish c. 1860

The first tenants of the Scottish row, doubtless accustomed to one-storey cottages, would have found it strange to go upstairs to sleep. These cottages form part of one of the planned villages of Morayshire. Anyone familiar with the houses of Scotland will at once notice that in designing them the architect has kept to the baronial tradition. He will note in particular, the dormer windows with their characteristically Scottish finials.

Cornish Fisherman's with Fore-stair c. 1850

This Victorian cottage is curiously alike in lay-out to the little mediaeval buildings today called King John's houses. Only the first floor, reached by steps outside, was used for living in: the owner felt safer up there. The lower storey, with a minimum of window space (sometimes none at all), was reserved for the storage of valuables. The mediaeval first-floor arrangement persists in the fishing villages of several counties – where nets are kept on the ground floor – and in the small towns of Scotland. It has often proved useful, of course, in areas liable to flooding by river or sea water.

Almshouse c. 1840

Victorian almshouses were customarily made externally imposing simply because that was how the benefactors who paid for
their erection wished it. One notes here the great square chimney
shafts set at an angle to their bases – this was a fashion for gentlemen's houses back in the seventeenth century – and the solid
Tudor-type porches with steeply pitched roofs. The inside is less
imposing: a row of small bed-sitting rooms for old people, each
having its own coal grate. The Victorians in general never tired of
resurrecting what they thought was the spirit of old England by
putting up imitations of buildings in the Tudor and other bygone
styles; but they made their doors and windows larger than the old
builders did, and their ceilings higher; they applied rich Tudor
detail to buildings whose scale would never have merited any
decoration at all at the earlier date.

There was thus no deliberate intention to deceive. In any case,
without the usual date stone, few observers would imagine for a
moment that a building like the one drawn was over 300 years old.
It is a Norfolk almshouse, but its counterparts are to be seen all
over England. The ecclesiastical look was thought suitable for
recipients of charity.

125

Farmworker's Terrace Type c. 1850

Despite their higher ceilings, some of the less pretentious mid-nineteenth-century cottages can be mistaken for eighteenth-century specimens. But a reaction to Georgian elegance is evident in a growing lack of concern for symmetry. A Georgian builder would never have constructed the drably irregular facade, suitable only for terraced cottages, which is shown here; the cottage appears, indeed to have been detached from a terrace. Nor, perhaps, would he have welcomed the improved products of the glass factories that made possible much larger panes. According to Mr M. W. Barley, whose photograph was used for the drawing, the chimney stack on the far gable end is a dummy.

Yorkshire Lead Miner's c. 1870

The Victorian builders became adept at putting up rather mean town cottages; most towns still have row upon row of them. But the type was not confined to the towns: the majority of late Victorian detached cottages are drearily urban, or at any rate alien to the rural tradition. This cottage on the Yorkshire moors is not more at ease in its open surroundings for being built of the local stone. Like the Lincolnshire one that precedes it, it seems to be a unit that could at any time form part of a terrace. However, as a single-depth building – that is, being only one room thick – it is a little closer to a rural origin.

Cumberland Longhouse c. 1870

The sash window, machine-cut slates and cement rendering had reached the Lake District by 1870, but a tradition of building cottages and barns in long low ranges persisted. Usually the buildings are to be seen beneath the same roof ridge. Upper-floored dwellings, too, were built as low as possible with the idea of escaping the worst of the winds in this exposed region. The unadorned, squat chimneys were equally practical; they were often protected against down draughts by two pieces of stone inclined together to form a V-shape.

Farmworker's Utility c. 1880

This snug box of brick and tile is a utility cottage set
down in a field in Kent and incised by the bricklayer 1877. The
front door opens on to a small kitchen with range, from which a
door immediately on the right leads to the parlour. A cased-in
staircase in this rooms leads up to a couple of bedrooms. The
overall shape is vaguely Georgian – if not the distribution of the
parts – and there is the feeling that the chimney stack and the door
strike a loose balance with the windows through being well to one
side in the opposite direction.

Jubilee Villas c. 1890

Except in hot countries the word villa was long ago devalued through over-use by speculative builders. In the late eighteenth century it meant a small, rather urban-looking country house of higher architectural merit than the farmhouse: there would usually be a pillared porch flanked by bay windows, and if possible a facade with a pediment. Rich parsons preferred villas as more fitting for the gentry, and office workers aspired to them. Inevitably they were gradually reduced in scale, rising up first in the suburbs of nineteenth-century towns and then on the outskirts of villages. Villa was a desirable label. By the 1870s it was being freely applied to semi-detached pairs.

The cement-faced cottages shown are typical of the so-called villas built in village surroundings. Each is two rooms deep, the front ground-floor room being the parlour, that little-used showpiece. The whole building is covered by a slated roof of wide single span. Behind there are low extensions to provide a place for the washing copper, the coal and the earth closet. Cottage plumbing, even in the numerous Jubilee Villas, was still rudimentary.

Index

Index

Cask, for slops, 58

Cattle sheds, 50

Ceilings, disadvantage of doing without, 66

Cement, Portland, 116, 128

Cesspools, contents of recommended for gardens, 52; overflowing into wells, 59

Chaps and chilblains, signs of more than mere exposure, 63

Charity, dwellings thought suitable for recipients of, 125

Charnwood Forest, 22

Chastity, near impossibility of, 37, 45

Chaucer, Geoffrey, 7

Cheap grain, 53

Chests, as family wardrobe, 37

Children, Poor Law arrangements for, 45; as labourers, 50

Chimney pots, 88; absence or sinking of, 107; formed with slips of stone, 108, 128

Chimney stacks, pride in ownership of, 10; as an afterthought, 80; central, 80, 87, 106; Cotswold with cornices, 85; as support for structure of a cottage, 87; external, 94; in end walls, 104, 108

Chippenham, 5

Church, attendance at, 36

Cisterns, rarity of, 61

Close stool, 14

Cobbett, William, 44, 115

Coke, Thomas, 32, 37

Colerne, squalor at, 5

Columella, 1779, Richard Graves, 29

Columns, simulated, 113

Concrete raft, 65

Confinements, 23

Consolations, in lives of poor cottagers, 42, 43

Coppers, lack of, 57; extensions for, 130

Cottagers, bracketed with paupers, 8; healthy, 43

Cottages, overcrowding of, 1, 7, 56, 60, 112; shared with animals, 50

poultry and so on, 1, 36, 42; as retreats for the well-to-do, 7; used as workshops, 36, 41; seen as cradles of population, 24; Act of 1589 against the erecting and maintaining of, 11, 21; sweet faces in, 42; for hinds, 44–5; often worse than stables, 50; disintegrating, 56; basic requirements for, 58; 'real bad', 63; worst ones at a distance from high roads, 64; lack of family seclusion, 64; experiments in cheap construction, 65; a three-bedroom dwelling for £110 (1913), 66; persistence of traditional designs, 69; extensions, 74; dating and its difficulties, 83, 86; companionship offered by the semi-detached, 104; pairs, 105; with living space above and storage below, 124; terrace construction applied to detached cottages; built low to escape winds, 128

Cottage types, weaver's, 41, 110; octagonal, 31, 116; cruck, 73; box frame, 75; box frame with concealed jetty, 77; balloon frame, 78, 79; plastered box frame, 80; Tudor house converted, 81; Cornish longhouse, 83; Cotswold limestone, 85; boarded box frame, 86; farmhouse type, 87, 106; western thatched, 88; eastern thatched, 89; economy timber, 90; Somerset stone, 91; rubble stone, 92; cob, 93; converted farmhouse, 95; subdivided, 96; Georgian-fronted vernacular, 97; Welsh traditional, 98; Essex verge, 99; Cornish vernacular, 100; estate foreman's popular, 101; brick and stud, 102; Norfolk farmworker's, 103; eastern semi-detached, 104; labourer's terrace, 105; transitional Georgian, 107; northern granite, 108; mansard-roofed semi, 109; Gothic revival lodge, 111, 114; model, 112; lock keeper's picturesque, 113; villas, 114, 121; work-

Index

Shutters, 74; as a means of deterring intruders, 77
Simond, L., 39
Sinks, metal, stone and cement, 58
Sketches in Architecture, 1798, Sir John Soane, 32
Slates, machine-cut, 108, 128
Sleeping arrangements, 1, 23; concern regarding the separation of boys and girls, 24; parents and six children in one bed, 26; indelicate habits encouraged by contiguity and mixed sleeping generally, 37
Sleeping lofts, reached by ladder, 92, 99
Slops, disposal of kitchen, 57–8, 62
Smith, George, 37
Smith, J. T., architectural historian, 76
Smith, J. T., artist, 4, 16, 20, 24
Smoke, dispersal from central hearth, 9, 10, 74; as a warming agent, 36; effect on decoration of cottages, 42; keeping doors open to get rid of, 58
Soane, Sir John, 32
Social worker, 58
Soot, an inch of on rafters, 9; everything made black and glossy by, 36
Softwood, wide use of Scandinavian for framework of cottages, 102, 119
South winds, alledged to bring the plague, 28
Southey, Robert, 5
Squatters, 11, 21; turf huts of, 37; their need to build in a great hurry, 22, 74
Stables and kennels, 23, 50
Stairs, semi-circular, 96; rarity in Scotland, 123; outside, 124; cased in, 129
Standpipe, 122
State of the Poor, The, 1746, Eden, 19
Stevens, Francis, 5
Strawberry Hill, 111
Stucco, 113–4; incised to resemble masonry, 115; its popularity, 115; use of Parker's Roman cement for, 116; considered dishonest, 116

Swaffam, 45
Sunday Times (1968), ix
Sutherland estates, Dark Age conditions on, 36
Symmetry in design, 15, 28, 32; demand for, 106; growing lack of concern about, 126

Tap, as a doubtful boon, 61
Task, The, 1784, William Cowper, 19
Tax, hearth, 8, 10, 41; window, 101, 107, 110; brick, 120
Taylor, John, the sailor poet, 12, 14
Teeth, neglect of, 55
Thatch, 4; snug appearance of, 17; eastern counties, 80; western counties, 89; reed, 89; wheat straw, 89; in scallops, 89; replaced by tiles, 96; need for a steep pitch, 103; forming gablets, 88, 105; on model cottages, 112; on picturesque cottages
Thieving, poaching, 8, 22
Thompson, Flora, 55
Thrift, poverty sometimes too acute for, 19
Tiles, patent Roman, 99; plain, 102, 103; pantiles, 103, 109
Timber, alleged shortage of, 78, 79; economy in use of, 79, 80, 90
Times, The (1898), 56, 93
Towns, the drift to, 53
Tranent, 1
Treaty of Paris, 31
Trevelyan, G. M., 49, 53
Tumbling, Dutch origin of, 104, 105

Undernourishment, 19, 58; as a reason for rapid onset of death in illness, 63
Union Chargeability Act, 56

Vegetables and herbs, 55
Verandahs, 47, 49
Vicar of Wakefield, The, 1766, Oliver Goldsmith, 17
Victoria, Queen, 2
Village, demolition of an entire, 34
Village Labourer, The, 1911, J. L. and